GOD'S LAST WORD TO MAN

GOD'S LAST WORD TO MAN

STUDIES IN HEBREWS

By
G. CAMPBELL MORGAN

WIPF & STOCK · Eugene, Oregon

Wipf and Stock Publishers
199 W 8th Ave, Suite 3
Eugene, OR 97401

God's Last Word to Man
Studies in Hebrews
By Morgan, G. Campbell
Copyright©1948 by Morgan, G. Campbell
ISBN 13: 978-1-608999-294-2
Publication date 2/18/2010
Previously published by Marshall Morgan & Scott, 1948

G. Campbell Morgan Reprint Series

Foreword

IF IT is true that the measure of a person's greatness is their influence, not only on his own time but on future generations, G. Campbell Morgan must be regarded as a great person. His greatness is seen not only in the wide impact of his ministry on both sides of the Atlantic, but in the fact that his books are still read and studied sixty-five years after his death. Named one of the ten greatest preachers of the twentieth-century by the contributing board of *Preaching* magazine, Morgan made the Bible a new and living book not only to the congregations who listened to him, but the vast multitude of persons who read his books.

Fox sixty-seven years Morgan preached and taught the Scriptures and served churches in England and the United States. What is remarkable is that his commentaries and expositions of the Bible still speak to persons of a new millennium. There have been many changes in the world since he faithfully preached and taught the Scriptures, but the wide appeal of his books testify to the timelessness of his message.

Although he held pastorates in the Congregational and Presbyterian denominations, he had an ecumenical appeal to persons of all denominations and traditions. The mystic Thomas á Kempis once wrote, "He to whom the eternal word speaks is delivered from many opinions." In one of his sermons, he referred to the words of Amos that there would be a famine for hearing the word of God (Amos 8:11). The timeless work of G. Campbell Morgan addresses that hunger, as his books enable his readers to get beyond opinions to the living Word.

Wipf and Stock Publishers have rendered a great gift to the religious world in reprinting dozens of Morgan's books. This growing collection makes his books more available, so that readers have an option other than searching the internet for used, and often expensive, copies. Among this collection is the classic *The Great Physician* and commentaries on the Gospel of Matthew and John. Persons seeking a living faith and a meaningful encounter with God would profit from reading any of these Morgan books.

Near the end of his ministry, in a sermon entitled "But One Thing," Morgan commented on how Portugal changed the words of a coin after Christopher Columbus discovered America. No longer did the inscription say, *Ne Plus Ultra* (nothing more beyond) but *Plus Ultra* (more beyond). It is the hope of the G. Campbell Morgan Trust that the reprinting of these books will bring readers to the "more beyond," and an even deeper encounter with the Word in Scripture.

THE MORGAN TRUST
Richard L. Morgan
Howard C. Morgan
John C. Morgan

CONTENTS

5

I

THE SON—GOD'S FINAL WORD TO MAN

" God, having of old time spoken unto the fathers in the prophets by divers portions and in divers manners, hath at the end of these days spoken unto us in His Son."—HEBREWS i. 1, 2a.

THE letter to the Hebrews has an especial value to-day because there is abroad a very widespread conception of Christ which is lower than that of the New Testament. To illustrate what I mean by this, a recent writer has said:

> " One of the best things we can say about human nature is this, that whenever a situation occurs which can only be solved by an individual ' laying down his life for his friends,' some heroic person is certain to come forth, sooner or later, and offer himself as the victim—a Curtius to leap into the gulf, a Socrates to drink the hemlock, a Christ to get himself crucified on Calvary."

I am not proposing to discuss that at any length, but at once say that to place Christ in that connection is to me little short of blasphemy. We may properly speak of " a Curtius," " a Socrates," but when we speak of " a Christ," our reference to Him is not only out of harmony with the New Testament presentation, but implicitly a contradiction of what it declares concerning the uniqueness of His Person.

7

When we turn to the letter to the Hebrews we have a presentation specially showing the separation of Christ from all others, and the reason of this is His Being and His work. Twice over in the course of the letter the writer calls upon his readers to "Consider Him." In the earlier occasion he says:

> "Consider the Apostle and High Priest of our confession";

and later on he says:

> "Consider Him that hath endured such gainsaying of sinners."

What is proposed in the present series of meditations is that we accept that challenge.

While it is self-evident that this letter or treatise was written to and for Hebrews, its teaching is for all Christians. The writer was evidently supremely conscious of the fact that the Hebrew people were created and chosen of God to be His instrument for reaching all nations; and while dealing with the great truth particularly from the standpoint of the Hebrew outlook, he was doing so in the interest of all those who were in the purpose of God. Therefore, while the letter is a Hebrew document, it is preëminently a human document; and so, while Christ is presented to us against the background of the Hebrew economy, He stands in the foreground clearly revealed as related to the purpose of God for humanity.

In the opening sentences of the book we are brought face to face with a philosophy, and a definite declaration. The philosophy is discovered in the assumptions of the writer which are clearly implicated, though not formally stated. The message is found in the declaration he makes on the basis of these assumptions.

The assumptions are two: first, God; and secondly, the fact that God speaks. The first assumption, that of the fact of God, is the assumption of the Biblical literature throughout. We cannot read the first sentence in Hebrews without being inevitably reminded of the first phrase in Genesis, " In the beginning God." Then and here, and indeed everywhere else, the fact of God is recognized, referred to, without any argument.

The second assumption is that this God makes Himself known to man—in other words, that He speaks. This at once necessarily presents God as more than an Energy diffused, or an Idea formulated; rather as having intelligence, and making known His thought to men. Later in the letter itself the writer says:

> " He that cometh to God must believe that He is, and that He is a Rewarder of them that seek after Him."

That statement follows the assumptions we have been referring to, namely, the existence of God, and the fact that He does approach men, and make Himself known.

As to the declarations, they are that God has spoken to men in history in two ways. We remind ourselves again that the letter was addressed to Hebrews, and of course to Hebrew Christians. Necessarily its outlook is limited by that fact. We may halt for a moment and take a wider outlook. There is no doubt that God spoke to other people than the Hebrew, and in other forms, which will account for certain elements of truth to be discovered in every form of religious thought. Nevertheless we believe that His supreme and central speech to all peoples came through the Hebrew people. From that standpoint, therefore, the writer, looking over human history, says:

" God, having of old time spoken unto the fathers,"

thus referring to the whole of the past economy; and continuing says:

" Hath at the end of these days spoken unto us in a Son."

If we survey the Old Testament literature, which gives us an account of what the writer refers to by the phrase, " of old time," we find that in His dealings with men, He is recorded as having spoken first through angels. No prophet or priest is found in Genesis. Then He spoke through leaders, Moses and Joshua. He never spoke to men directly as to His government through kings. Then came the prophets. We shall find all these referred to in the course of this letter. The argument of the writer passes in review these methods of the past—angels, leaders, priests, and prophets.

We may survey the letter by imagining a Hebrew Christian reading it, and finding an answer to the things he might be inclined to say if or when, per-chance, he was tempted to think that in passing from

the splendid ritual of the Mosaic economy to the
simplicity found in Christ, something vital was lost.
He might say, for instance, The things of our religion
were ministered by angels. Says the writer in reply,
That is true, but the Son is greater than the angels.
But, says the Hebrew Christian again, We had a great
leader from God, Moses. That, says the writer, is
equally true, but he was a servant in the house, and the
Son is greater than the servant; and moreover, Moses,
while leading the people out, was unable to lead them
into possession. That being granted, says the Hebrew,
Joshua led us into the land. He did, says the writer,
but he could give you no rest. The Son not only leads
out, but leads in, and gives rest. Continuing, the
Hebrew might refer to the great priesthood and rit-
ualistic system of the past. This, the writer replies in
effect, is all true, and was divinely arranged, but it
made nothing perfect; and the coming of the Son was
the coming of the Priest with the better covenant, and
the better worship. And yet once more, the Hebrew
might say, We had prophets who spoke to us the Word
of God. That is true is the argument of the letter
writer, but all they said was partial. The Word of God
through the Son is full and final. Thus it is seen that
the opening declaration that God spoke in times past
in divers portions and manners is recognized throughout as being true. God certainly was making Himself
and His way known to men through all the period. But
at last, after the days of diversity and processional
method, during which so much had been said, but the
final word had not been uttered, He spoke in His Son.

The question arises in the mind as to the reason why
God adopted this method of dealing with men. We
may find help in words on another occasion, which our
Lord Himself uttered to His disciples at the end of His
ministry, namely:

> "I have yet many things to say unto you, but ye
> cannot bear them now."

From these words we see that the Divine method is
always characterized by a process and a progression.
God had in the past many things to say to men, but He
only said them as man was able to bear them. This
continued until the time when God spoke to men in His
Son; and the difference between the past and this, is
the difference between the processional and the final.
The finality of the speech of God to men through His
Son is thus suggested in the opening sentences, and
argued for through the whole of the writing. Here it
should be said that while the speech of the Son was
final, man has not finally apprehended that speech.
Still the method is as man is able to bear; but now the
process under the guidance of the Spirit of truth is
that of the interpretation of the final speech of God.

Now we turn to consider the One referred to as " the
Son." In the opening paragraph we have a sevenfold
description of " the Son." He is first " Heir of all
things " ; secondly, " through Whom He fashioned the
ages " ; thirdly, in Himself He is " the Effulgence " of
the Divine glory; fourthly, He is " the very Image of
His substance," that is of the essence of Deity; fifthly,
He is spoken of as " upholding all things by the word

of His power," a reference to the maintenance of the moral order; sixthly, He is revealed in redeeming activity, making "purification of sins"; finally, His administrative position is declared, "He sat down at the right hand of the Majesty on High." That seven-fold description is completed by another statement, perfecting the octave of the revelation. We are told that presently He will come again into the economy, and that when He does so, all the angels shall worship Him.

To accept this interpretation of the Son is never to be able to say, here "a Curtius," and there "a Socrates," and here "a Christ." This presentation of Him puts Him out of comparison with all others.

This Son is first declared to be appointed by God, "Heir of all things"; and in that connection the statement is made that through Him the ages have been fashioned, a declaration revealing Him as over-ruling all the movements in human history. Passing from these declarations concerning His position, the writer speaks of the essential fact of His Being, and declares that He is "the Effulgence" of the Divine glory—that is, the One through Whom there was an out-flowing of that glory into manifestation. That being so, continuing, He is described as "the very Image of His substance." The margin of the Revised Version suggests that we should substitute for the word "image" the word "impress." The idea plainly is that the underlying mystery of Deity which cannot be grasped or finally interpreted by human intellect, was seen in the Son. Returning from this sublime refer-

ence to His Being, the writer next says of Him, " upholding all things by the word of His power." This
reference, of course, may refer to the material order of
the universe, as Paul says all things consist or hold
together in Him; but I tend to the belief that the reference is rather to the word of moral authority. Once
more, in what is but a passing reference, the redeeming
mystery of the Cross is recognized in the words, " when
He had made purification of sins " ; until finally it is
declared that having done that, " He sat down at the
right hand of the Majesty on High."

This is the Christ; this is the Son; this is the One
through Whom God has now spoken. Having thus
described Him, the writer looking on says, " When He
again bringeth in the Firstborn into the world." Here
is one of the sentences where the translators have
rendered a Greek word by the word " world," and the
Revisers suggest in the margin that instead of " world "
we should read " the inhabited earth." I submit that
it would be far better to transliterate the Greek word,
and allow the sentence to read, " When He again
bringeth in the Firstborn into the economy." That
word " economy " was in common use in the time of
our Lord, and of the writers of the New Testament as
referring to the Roman Empire. Now, says this writer,
the Son is. coming again into the economy which He
established, and when He comes, all angels will worship
Him. This is the Son through Whom God has spoken,
and is still speaking.

Let me conclude the present meditation by re-
emphasizing things said at its commencement. When

God spoke to men in Christ He said everything He had to say, which means that He said everything man needs to hear for his earthly life. I am careful to put it in that way, because there are things not said in Christ during the present life. Paul said in writing to the Corinthians, " Now we know in part," and the one thing certain is that in Christ we may know all we need to know for today. To that statement I should like to add that even in the ages to come we shall still find, as I believe, all our knowledge centred in Him, as it increases.

To return, however, to that limited idea, we inquire, What are the things man needs to know? That is What are the things essential for the well-being of human nature? I should answer that the first is authority. There is nothing the world needs today more than authority; but it must be an authority that carries the consent of the governed. Human methods have constantly been those of coercing men to do things without their own consent. This always ulti-mately breaks down. When God spoke in the Son He gave men the one King, Who, being known in Himself, Whose words being rightly apprehended, man will find the authority to which he can yield himself with perfect agreement.

This very finality of authority brings with it a sense of failure, and out of this arises the next element of human need. It is that of a Mediator or Arbiter, Who shall come between God and man, and act so as to bring about a reconciliation. This is perfectly provided in the Son.

Once more, having found the King Whose standards condemn us, and the Priest Whose redemption reconciles us, we now need a Prophet Who can lead us progressively and unfailingly along all the ways of life. That Prophet is found in the Son.

II

THE SON—HIGHER THAN THE ANGELS

" And of the angels He saith,
Who maketh His angels winds,
And his ministers a flame of fire;
but of the son He saith,
Thy throne, O God, is for ever and ever."
—HEBREWS i. 7, 8a.

THE finality of the speech of God to man through
the Son is, as we have seen, the burden of the letter
to the Hebrews, and that finality of speech is proven
by the writer as he claims the preëminence of the Son
over all those through whom God in the earlier period
had spoken to men. The fact that He had spoken is
definitely declared, and that He had done so in " divers
portions and divers manners." After the period in
which He thus spoke, He now spoke again, and that
in His Son; and in doing so, said all that He has to
say to man.

As we recognized in our previous meditation, the
literature of the Old Testament records God's speaking to men through angels, through leaders, through
priests, and through prophets. Through all these there
had come to man authentic messages from God, but
they were all partial, and therefore incomplete. Now

He has spoken in His Son, and the arguments of the letter are intended to show how that speech is final by reason of the absolute superiority of the Son to angels, leaders, priests, prophets.

Our present consideration is concerned with the first movement in the argument which deals with the superiority of the Son to the angels. The writer deals with this by a remarkable selection of quotations from the Old Testament, that is from the literature recording what God had said, " of old time." There are seven such distinct quotations, and they are grouped in order to enforce the truth of the superiority of the Son to angels. Throughout, the dignity of the angels is recognized, but that of the Son is seen to be infinitely greater. We may follow the argument by considering first the angels, and then the Son.

We are living at a time when the idea of angels is being discounted or dismissed, perhaps by smiling at it as moving in the realm of fairy stories. Of course, in common with all modern views, that is an ancient view. The Sadducees, we are distinctly told, did not believe in angels. I am not proposing to argue for their existence, but to recognize it as a fact upon the authority of the Biblical Literature both in the Old and New Testaments. In the Old we have certain clear statements concerning their activities, and that is equally true of the New.

It is of interest to pause here and remind ourselves of what the New Testament tells us about the relation of angels to the earthly ministry of Jesus. It was an angel that made the great announcement to the Virgin

Mother. Angels sang at the birth of the Babe. Angels ministered to Him when He had been with the wild beasts in the wilderness temptation. Again they drew near and ministered to Him in Gethsemane. There is no reference to them in connection with the Cross. There He was alone. When the resurrection morning broke, angels were once more there to tell the story to earth.

The question may arise at this point as to why angels are not now seen. One reply to that may properly be that as messengers of God to men, they are no longer necessary, seeing that He has said everything He has to say in His Son. At the same time we must not forget that the New Testament distinctly speaks of them as " ministering spirits, sent forth to do service for the sake of them that shall inherit salvation." In that remarkable book, *Something Happened*, giving an account of some of the experiences of Mildred Cable and Evangeline and Francesca French, they tell of how once being on the edge of the Gobi Desert, in the hands of bandits, they went into their little tent and lay down, not knowing what was going to happen on the human level. They tell how they watched the bandits underneath the tent for a little while, and then this sentence occurs:

" After a while they slept, and the angels took charge."

Of course that may be dismissed by some as the poetic imagination of a woman. That, however, does not invalidate the story, for one remembers how something like that was said, according to the New Testament, immediately after the resurrection:

> " Certain women of our company . . . came saying that they had also seen a vision of angels."

It is impossible to read that without discovering in it the note of incredulity, and perhaps for the same reason.

Angels, according to these Biblical records, were the first intermediaries between God and man after man's revolt from the Divine government. In the records found in the book of Genesis no outstanding leader appears, no priest is found, no prophet is heard. In all those early periods of human history, the direct messages of God were brought to men through angels. There is one story which seems an exception. Once a king is seen who is also a priest. This is Melchizedek. Quite evidently the story is unique in that period, and without entering into the matter here and now fully, as we shall reach it in later studies, I may at least say that I have long been convinced that the appearing of Melchizedek was a Christophany.

In his dealing with this matter, the writer describes the angels first thus:

> " Who maketh His angels winds,
>   And His ministers a flame of fire."

Unquestionably the marginal rendering should be adopted:

> " Who maketh His angels spirits."

In this quotation we find a recognition of their glory and of their nature. Their activity is described by the writer in words we have already referred to:

"Are they not all ministering spirits, sent forth to do service?"

The King James's Version reads:

"Are they not all ministering spirits, sent forth to minister?"

The Revisers, by rendering "sent forth to do service," have intended to draw attention to a difference between the two verbs made use of. This is an important matter, because we have a revelation of the twofold work of the angels. The first word, rendered "ministering," by transliteration might be rendered "liturgical." Ministering spirits are liturgical spirits, that is, those whose one supreme service is that of worshipping God, and offering praise to Him. They veil their faces in the presence of the ineffable glory, and celebrate the holiness of God. We have a radiant illustration of that in Isaiah vi., where the seraphim are seen worshipping, acting as liturgical spirits.

But they have another mission. They are sent forth. Sometimes under the authority of God they cease their worship, and are sent forth to minister. This is also seen in the story in Isaiah already referred to. When at the vision of the glory the young prophet became conscious of himself as by comparison unclean, and cried:

"Woe is me! for I am undone; because I am a man
of unclean lips, and I dwell in the midst of a people
of unclean lips,"

then immediately

"Flew one of the seraphim unto me, having a live
coal in his hand."

Thus the seraph was sent forth to minister. Thus the
writer, by reference to the past, recognizes the glory
of the angels, and the sacredness of their mission as
messengers of God to men. This recognition makes all
the more forceful the revelation of the finality of the
speech of the Son, as He is seen in inherent and necessary superiority to angels.

Now let us glance over these seven quotations. Five
of them are taken from the Book of Psalms; one
arrestingly, from Samuel, and one from the Book of
Deuteronomy.

The first two are found in the fifth verse of chapter
one, and they deal with the office and nature of the
Son. The writer points out that when the Psalmist
wrote that song, he was referring to a fulfilment which
came in Jesus, and speaking of the method of address:

"Thou art My Son,
This day have I begotten Thee,"

points out by interrogation that such designation was
never used of angels. They are ever servants, worshipping and serving. The Son is in authority by
Divine decree.

It is in that connection, very arrestingly, that he quotes from Samuel words which in their first application were used of Solomon:

> " I will be to Him a Father,
> And He shall be to Me a Son."

Evidently this writer saw that the history of the Old Testament was prophetic, and that such words could only come to complete fulfilment in the actual Son of God. In this specific sense no angel can be so described.

The third quotation is taken from the Septuagint Version of the Old Testament:

> " And let all the angels of God worship Him."

This the writer applies to the time when God will " again " bring " in the Firstborn into the world."

The word " world " here is rendered in the margin " the inhabited earth." The actual word is the Greek word which may be correctly transliterated " economy." Whatever the time reference may be, the writer is showing that the angels are called upon to worship the Son. They exercise the highest function of their being, that of worship offered to the Son. This again is a quotation, emphasizing the measureless distance between the Son and angels.

In the fourth, fifth, and sixth quotations, the writer is contrasting the service of the angels with the supremacy of the Son. They serve gloriously, but they serve. The Son exercises the rule of God.

> " Thy throne, O God, is for ever and ever,
>   And the sceptre of uprightness is the sceptre of
>   Thy Kingdom."

Continuing the quotation, he describes the nature of that rule:

> " Thou hast loved righteousness, and hated iniquity;
>   Therefore God, Thy God, hath anointed Thee
>   With the oil of gladness above Thy fellows."

The glorious company of the angels and archangels, cherubim and seraphim, are all seen as rendering worship to the Son.

Still continuing his quotations the writer shows the Son as not only exercising the rule of God, but co-operating with God in creation:

> " Thou, Lord, in the beginning hast laid the founda-
>   tion of the earth,
>   And the heavens are the works of Thy hands."

Further, he shows the Son as sharing the eternity of God. Referring to all created things, he says:

> " They shall perish; but Thou continuest;
>   And they all shall wax old as doth a garment;
>   And as a mantle shalt Thou roll them up,
>   As a garment, and they shall be changed;
>   But Thou art the same,
>   And Thy years shall not fail."

The final quotation describes the preëminent position of the Son:

" But of which of the angels hath He said at any time,
Sit Thou on My right hand,
Till I make thine enemies the footstool of thy feet? "

Here the Son is seen as finally enthroned, and waiting
in that position for the ultimate subjugation of all
enemies to His rule.

This interpretation of the Person and position of the
Son demonstrates the finality of the speech of God
through Him, and gives force to the exhortation and
warning found in the first four verses of chapter two:

" Therefore we ought to give the more earnest heed
to the things that were heard, lest haply we drift away
from them. For if the word spoken through angels
proved stedfast, and every transgression and disobedience received a just recompense of reward; how shall
we escape, if we neglect so great salvation? which
having at the first been spoken through the Lord, was
confirmed unto us by them that heard; God also bearing witness with them, both by signs and wonders, and
by manifold powers, and by gifts of the Holy Spirit,
according to His own will."

Christianity is not a quest after truth. Procession-
ally it is an investigation of the truth which in totality
came from God to man through Him Who said, " I
am the Truth." In His high service the angels are still
employed as liturgical spirits, worshipping; and as
ministering spirits, serving " them that shall inherit
salvation."

Whereas we may be, and assuredly are among those
whom the angels serve under the command of the Son,

we do not need their mediation, or their messages, for knowledge of the will of God. That is perfectly revealed in Him through Whom His final speech has come to man.

III

THE SON—LOWER THAN THE ANGELS— CROWNED

" But we behold Him Who hath been made a little lower than the angels, even Jesus, because of the suffering of death crowned with glory and honour, that by the grace of God He should taste death for every man."—HEBREWS ii. 9.

THE section of the letter in which these words are found follows closely upon that in which the writer had been dealing with the superiority of the Son to angels, and stands in startling contrast to it. He Who by virtue of His nature and oneness with God in absolute sovereignty, is infinitely higher than the angels, is now presented as made lower than the angels. All the values of the section are focused in the words of the text, which, however, necessarily needs the context for its interpretation.

The opening words:

" For not unto the angels did He subject the world to come, whereof we speak,"

will be understood better if it be rendered:

" Not unto the angels did He subject the economy to come."

The Greek word *oikoumene*, rendered " world " in our

translations, and by suggestion, " the inhabited earth " in the margin, is, of course, the word from which our word economy is derived. In Luke's account of our Lord's temptation the same word is employed when he tells us that the devil showed Him all the kingdoms of the economy. The world at the time was in common use in reference to the whole Roman Empire. Glancing back in this letter to chapter one, verse six, we read:

> " When He again bringeth in the Firstborn into the world."

Here it is the same word, and might more helpfully be rendered:

> " When He again bringeth in the Firstborn into the economy."

The reference there was unquestionably to the second Advent, and the declaration is that then all the angels of God worship Him. In the present section, referring to the same economy, the writer says:

> " The economy to come, whereof we speak."

Taking the word then as referring to the Kingdom of God in its perfection, he says that that is not to be subjected to the angels. We remember that this letter was written to Hebrews, and that the will of God had been made known to men in the patriarchal periods through angels. The Hebrew people had come to believe that angels were the special guardians of their national life, and warrant for this view may be found

in the sacred Scriptures.   The writer of the letter is
pointing out that in the new economy, resulting from
the final speech of God to men, this will no longer be
the case.   That economy will be solely under the
dominion of the Son.

It is here that the startling statement of the text
occurs, in which he speaks of the Son as having been
made lower than the angels, and the reason for that is
that He may obtain and exercise this final dominion.

Once more our Version reads:

" We behold Him Who hath been made a little lower
than the angels."

Here it is important to understand that the word
" little " does not refer to a degree, but to a period of
time.   We catch its true significance if we render it:

" Made for a little while lower than the angels."

Thus we are brought face to face with the central
wonder and majesty of our holy religion.   He Who
by virtue of His Being and His nature, and His consequent relationship with the absolute Sovereignty of
Deity, is higher than the angels, is for a little while
made lower than the angels.

This descent of the Son to a position lower than the
angels is dealt with by the writer first by a reference
to human nature.   The reference opens with the words,
" One hath somewhere testified," and consists of a
quotation from Hebrew psalmody:

> " What is man, that Thou art mindful of him?
> Or the son of man, that Thou visitest him?
> Thou madest him a little lower than the angels;
> Thou crownedst him with glory and honour,
> And didst set him over the works of Thy hands;
> Thou didst put all things in subjection under
> his feet."

That quotation is intended to show the dignity of human nature. Having made the quotation, in one brief and pregnant sentence, he declares the failure of humanity:

> " We see not yet all things subjected to him."

In that statement the word " him " refers to man.

It is well that we halt to consider that revelation of the dignity of man in itself. Whereas the writer does not quote the words, the Psalmist began:

> " When I consider Thy heavens, the work of Thy
> fingers,
> The moon and the stars, which Thou hast
> ordained,
> What is man, that Thou art mindful of him?
> And the son of man, that Thou visitest him? "

In asking these questions the singer was conscious first of the apparent insignificance of man in the presence of the wonders of the universe, but he was also conscious of something in man which set him on a higher level than anything to be found amid those stupendous wonders. The thought filling his mind was concerned with the mysterious majesty of man. Perchance singing out of a personal consciousness, he found himself, by comparison, insignificant amid the splendours of the universe, and yet was conscious that God was mindful of him, and visited him.

Still referring to man, he declared that he was made for a little while lower than the angels. Man was seen then as lower in rank than angels, but only for a little while. The implicate is that in the Divine purpose for man ultimately, he is to be lifted into a position higher than the angels. Confessedly this is a great conception of human nature. It may be said that one phase of the terrible malady from which humanity suffers is that he thinks of himself more meanly than God thinks of him. It is this dignity according to the Divine ideal, which fits man for the exercise of dominion:

> " Thou didst set him over the works of Thy hands;
> Thou didst put all things in subjection under his feet."

In order to the ultimate realization of the meaning of his being, man was placed on the level of disciplinary probation.

As we survey human history, we see two things clearly marked. One is man's failure to realize and exercise completely this power of dominion; and the other is the constant movement towards victory in that direction. His dominion has been growingly extended over the earth, over the sea, over the air. As a writer some while ago put it, " Man is learning to master everything except himself." In all the victories won, man is seen as to his potentiality, and as to the Divine purpose for him.

The failure of man is recognized then by the writer of this letter when he says:

" We see not yet all things subjected to him."

The reason of this failure, as the whole of the Biblical literature reveals and emphasizes, is that of man's revolt against the government of God.

All this leads to the writer's introduction of the word " Jesus," as he declares that while it is true we do not see all things subjected to man:

" We behold Him . . . even Jesus."

Here again two words occur which arrest our attention, both referring to vision, but having variety of suggestion. " We see not," and " we behold." The first is the word which is general and inclusive. The second is a word which suggests intensive observation. Thus he draws attention to this One, at the centre of human history, linked with the humanity that has failed, but standing separated from it.

This One Whom He speaks of as Lord, and now names " Jesus," is declared to be One made for a little while lower than the angels. That in the first instance means that He has passed the angels, and touched our level.

If, however, we pause there, we fall short of understanding the ultimate value of that descent. Therefore, continuing our reading, we find the reason of the descent declared in the words:

"Because of the suffering of death, crowned with glory and honour, that by the grace of God He should taste death for every man."

Thus it is clearly revealed that the ultimate purpose of the Incarnation was not that of the revelation of an ideal. The Son was made lower than the angels, descending to the level of human nature, in order that He might die. From death angels are exempt, therefore He passed them by, coming not merely to the level of ideal humanity, but to the level of failing humanity; made lower than the angels that He might taste death.

In this connection, however, the writer utters something so arresting and sublime that were it not the word of inspired interpretation, we should never have dared to imagine it. I refer to the terms in which he speaks of this very fact. While declaring that the Son was made lower than the angels because of the suffering of death, and that the intention of the descent was that He should die, he speaks of the whole thing as a coronation, saying that He was

"Crowned with glory and honour, that by the grace of God He should taste death for every man."

The statement is not that He was crowned with glory and honour because He tasted death, but rather that He was crowned with glory and honour in order that He might taste death. The amazing and revealing declaration then is that God conferred upon His eternal Son a crown of glory when He gave Him to death for the ransom of a race.

Thus, in being made lower than the angels for a little while, He came into identification with man not only in the essential ideal of His nature, but in all the suffering and the sin which resulted from man's failure. It is in this connection that the writer says:

> " He that sanctifieth and they that are sanctified
>   are all of one,
> For which cause He is not ashamed to call them
>   brethren, saying,
>   I will declare Thy name unto My brethren,
>   In the midst of the congregation will I sing
>   Thy praise."

This quotation is taken from the twenty-second Psalm, which begins with the cry which was uttered by our Lord on the Cross:

> " My God, My God, why hast Thou forsaken Me? "

In that Psalm the Messianic sorrows are set forth, but they are revealed as leading to the declaration of victory wherein the suffering One will declare God's name to His brethren, with the result of the song of praise which will ascend to God.

Thus God's final speech to man through the Son, Who is higher than the angels, has come to him because He descended on to the human level, and passed through the bitterness of death, the ultimate dereliction; in order that He Himself might ascend to His place higher than the angels, making a way by which man who had fallen from his high estate, might regain everything that he had lost.

This is the perpetual message of the New Testament concerning the Son. The music is heard throughout in varying tones, sometimes major and sometimes minor; all merging in the ultimate speech of God, which tells man of His eternal love, and of the way by which man may be redeemed.

IV

THE SON—GREATER THAN MOSES

" Moses indeed was faithful in all His House as a servant, for a testimony of those things which were afterward to be spoken; but Christ as a Son, over His House."—HEBREWS iii. 5, 6a.

God had spoken to His ancient people through Moses. The authority of the message through Moses had been undoubted. It was the conviction that God had spoken through him which had created and kept the nation through all the running centuries. It is perfectly natural, therefore, that Moses was held in great veneration. As an instance of that veneration it may be stated that some of the old Rabbis declared that there were fifty gates to wisdom, and that Moses held the key to all save one. It was, of course, merely a rabbinical saying, but it reveals the veneration in which he was held.

The writer of this letter is careful not to undermine the authority of Moses, or to minimize it in any way. His argument is intended to show that those who hear the speech of the Son hear something which has yet greater authority than Moses, because it is a final message.

The section dealing with this matter commences with a call:

36

"Wherefore, holy brethren, partakers of a heavenly calling, consider the Apostle and High Priest of our confession, even Jesus."

The "Wherefore" of the call refers to all that had already been written. Because of the superiority of the Son to angels, and because He had been made lower than the angels, in order to rise to a yet fuller authority, and open the way for others to follow Him, we are called upon to

"Consider the Apostle and High Priest of our confession, even Jesus."

The word "Consider" is an arresting and significant one. Towards the end of the letter we shall find it occurs again in another application. The word calls for careful attention with serious thought, such now to be occupied with Jesus as the "Apostle and High Priest of our confession." The word "Apostle" is used here in its simplest sense, as referring to One set apart and sent by God; and the word "High Priest" refers to One mediating between God and man by Divine appointment.

Having uttered the call, the writer proceeded to deal with the superiority of the Son to Moses. In order to understand his teaching it is necessary that we have a clear view of the background of the argument, and of the authority and greatness of Moses. Let it at once be emphasized anew that the argument does not compare Jesus as the One Who did not fail with Moses as one who did fail; but rather as One Who essentially was greater even than the one who was great in his service. It is quite true that at certain points Moses failed as the records reveal. No reference, however, here is made to failure, but rather to fidelity. Over against his fidelity, however, the writer shows that the speech of the Son is greater as to final authority than anything Moses, even in his faithfulness, had ever said.

When I speak of the background I refer to the fact that in this brief passage in which the writer is fixing attention upon Moses and upon Jesus, he has an outlook upon something with which both Moses and Jesus had relationship. The inclusive outlook is revealed in the recurrence in the passage seven times over of the word " house." If we glance down the paragraph we shall find that the word " house " is preceded by the pronoun " His " three times, and " Whose " once. These pronouns do not refer to Moses, but to God. Attention is drawn to this fact in the margin of the Revised Version. The background, then, of the whole argument is that of the House of God, in which Moses was a servant, and Jesus a Son. This House is referred to as being built, the exact meaning of the word there being established, or equipped, which, of course, postulates an act of building also. The idea, then, is that of a House built, established, equipped.

What, then, is the House of God thus referred to? We call to mind how in school days, when considering the history of England, we became familiar with the terms, House of Plantagenet, House of Tudor, House of Stuart, and so on. The reference was in each case to kings, but included the idea of the realm over which

they reigned. The term, then, "the House of God,"
refers to the Divine Kingship, and the economy or
order resulting from its exercise. This repeated reference to the House of God has that in mind; the government of God, and all that results therefrom. The
writer is conscious of the sovereignty of God, and of
the results of that sovereignty in the order established
by all such as are submitted thereto.

This, then, is the background, the unifying and
inclusive outlook. In that House Moses served, while
over it Jesus rules as Son. This complete vision, therefore, is that of the persistent reign of God, including
Hebraism and Christianity, not antagonistic to each
other, but constituting two stages in the building up
of the Divine order. In our Bible we have what we
speak of as the Old Testament and the New Testament; and we think of the Mosaic dispensation and
the Christian dispensation as separated from each
other. While that is true in a sense, the larger truth
is that of the one Kingdom, or House of God, spanning
human history and including both dispensations.

In that whole, Moses is seen in his greatness as the
servant of God. Here once more we are halted by a
word. In our New Testament we have two different
words which are both rendered "servant." One is
doulos, and the other *diakonos; doulos* strictly meaning a bond-servant, and the other a servant who runs
on errands. Neither of these words is employed by the
writer of the letter to describe Moses. The word used
here is *therapon*, which signifies one who renders
voluntary service inspired by affection. *Doulos* might

have been used, for Moses was certainly in a sense a bond-servant of Jehovah. *Diakonos* certainly might have been used, for he was ever running on the errands of God. Nevertheless the writer deliberately chooses a word which lifts service on to a higher level than can be suggested by either of the other words. Thus the very word employed emphasizes the greatness of Moses.

Moreover, he is distinctly referred to as one appointed by God, and it is declared that he was faithful in all the House of God. This faithfulness, moreover, was by the writer declared to be in order to

"A testimony of those things which were afterward to be spoken."

In this final declaration there is a recognition of the fact that the service of Moses was not in itself final, but preliminary, leading on to something more yet to be said.

When we look back at the history of Moses we see how he served in the House of God. That service was rendered in the building of the Tabernacle according to the pattern given. In that Tabernacle every detail was symbolic, and intended so to be. Everything was a testimony of those things to be spoken afterwards. God spoke through His servant Moses in His House in all the ceremonial ritual, so full of ornate splendour.

And yet again, Moses was the faithful servant in his reception of the law, and his interpretation of it to the people. As Moses had said:

"Jehovah, thy God, hath spoken all these words,"

referring to the ten words of the Decalogue; and
equally to all the interpretation of those words found
in the laws given to the people, in detail. Thus Moses
stands out in all his greatness, a greatness which is
recognized by this writer.

With this recognition the writer puts Christ into
sharp contrast with Moses as he speaks of Him as
being " a Son over His own House." Moses and Jesus
were appointed by God. Both were faithful; Moses
as a servant voluntarily, and love-inspired; Jesus as
also a Servant faithful, but as a Son in authority.

Being thus a Son, He is also the Builder of the
House, and this applies to all that in which Moses
served, as well as to all that which issued from the
Advent of the Son in human history. In every process
of the past, in which the greatness of Moses was manifested as he served, the Son Himself was the Builder.

And not the Builder only, but the Ruler. In His
building and in His rule, the economy of God was
carried forward until it finds its manifestation in the
new economy which historically and manifestly is that
of the Son. This is evident in the words of the writer:

> " Whose House are we, if we hold fast our boldness
> and the glorying of our hope firm unto the end."

Thus the whole Divine movement in history is seen,
the period in which Moses served, as it merged into
what we may describe as the distinctly Christian
period, composed of

> " Holy brethren, partakers of a heavenly calling,"

the House of God today, which is the Church of God.

The Son, superior to angels, made lower than the angels for the suffering of death, is seen at last in the full and final authority of His relationship to God. Because of this fact, Moses, great as he was, is entirely superseded. That does not mean that anything that fell from the lips of Moses, either in material symbolism or in interpretation of the law, was abrogated. Our Lord Himself, with great definiteness, declared:

"I came not to destroy, but to fulfil the law and the prophets."

What is intended is that through the Son, everything symbolized in the ritual, and everything demanded in the law finds fulfilment.

We may then, in conclusion, observe the comparisons between what Moses had said authoritatively as a servant, and what the Son has said in full and final authority as the Builder and Ruler of the House of God. The comparison is between Moses and Jesus in the method of the Divine approach to man.

Everything is summarized in the Prologue of the Gospel according to John in words full of majesty, and characterized by simplicity:

"The law came through Moses; grace and truth came through Jesus Christ."

The writer does not suggest that there was nothing of grace in the Mosaic economy, but rather that it was not clearly manifest. Neither does he suggest that there is nothing of law in the economy of the Son, for the word " truth " includes all of law.

Included within this comparison is that of the ethical demands of Moses and of Jesus. The laws which came from God through Moses were laws of conduct. In the enunciation of law from the lips of the Son on the Mount of Beatitudes, conduct was certainly referred to; but all the demands were demands on character. The laws of Moses were laws conditioning the doing of things. The laws of Jesus demanded being, or a condition of heart:

> " Blessed are the pure in heart, for they shall see God."

To face the ethical demands of Jesus, apart from His saving grace, is to be filled with a sense of unutterable failure.

Thus we reach the final thought of comparison, that of the approach of God to man through Moses, and the approach of God to man through Jesus. The difference may be discovered by the reading of the twentieth chapter of Exodus in close connection with the twenty-seventh chapter of Matthew, which, of course, simply means the comparison between Sinai and Calvary.

Through Moses, God spoke to men in thunder, in cloud, in lightning, in the terror of tempest, and earthquake. Through Jesus He spoke through a broken, bruised and dying Man Who was infinitely more than Man. By Sinai came the law. By Calvary came the flowing of the river of grace.

The speech, then, of the Son is proved final, as we contemplate the superb greatness of Moses as a servant, marked by fidelity; and then turn our eyes to the One Who, as Son, is at once Builder of the House, and Ruler of the House. Through Him God today speaks to man.

V

THE SON—GREATER THAN MOSES,
" WHEREFORE "

*"Take heed, brethren, lest haply there shall be in any one of you
an evil heart of unbelief, in falling away from the living God."*
—HEBREWS iii. 12.

THESE words occur in a passage of warning and
exhortation (Heb. iii. 5–19). A characteristic of this
letter is that the writer constantly turned aside from
the main line of argument to utter such words. The
warning here is focused in the words of the text.
These words are more immediately connected with the
paragraph beginning with the word " Wherefore " in
the seventh verse. Between that word and this particular injunction is a quotation taken from Psalm
ninety-five. This quotation had reference to the
experience of the Hebrew people in the wilderness during their tarrying there for forty years, under the
direct leadership of Moses. Consequently the warning
is closely connected with the claim that the writer had
made, that Jesus was greater than Moses.

The letter was written to those who had been under
Moses, the God-given leader, but who now were under
the Son, God's final Leader. Having shown the
superiority of the Son, even over the faithfulness of
Moses, these words of warning were written. The

45

illustrations he takes are not of the failure of Moses, but of the failure of the people to obey him. Moses was faithful, but the people had been disobedient. The words, therefore, consist of a solemn warning to such as have the greater Leadership of the Son, lest they also should fail in like manner.

From this brief examination of the surrounding passage we may turn to the warning itself. God has spoken through His Son. God has given Him—to quote the ancient prophecy—to be "A Leader and Commander to the people." Therefore let us "take heed." In this warning two matters arrest our attention, first that of the danger described; "falling away from the living God"; and secondly, the process through which this falling away may take place, "an evil heart of unbelief."

Whereas we should remember that the letter was addressed to all those who are described as "holy brethren, partakers of a heavenly calling," everything in the warning is reduced to the terms of the individual:

> "Lest there should be in *any one of you* an evil heart of unbelief, in falling away from the living God."

We are ever prone to miss the whole force of teaching directed to the saints generally, or to the whole Church. It is well, therefore, that we consider it as an individual word in a personal way. The strength of the aggregate is created by the loyalty of the individual. A chain is only as strong as its weakest link. A castle is only as safe as its least guarded door. The strength of the Church is created by the loyalties of its members. Thus the writer arrests us individually in the words, " Lest . . . any one of you."

The peril then is described as " Falling away from the living God." The arresting phrase is " the living God." In itself it reveals the distinguishing conception of the Hebrew people. The one central conviction of that people from the father of the nation, Abraham, was the Monotheistic conviction, the fact that there is one God. But more than that; they ever thought of Him as "the living God." Their prophets and poets in referring to other religions, as contrasted with that centred in Jehovah, spoke of false gods as dead:

> " They have mouths, but they speak not;
> Eyes have they, but they see not;
> Noses have they, but they smell not;
> They have hands, but they handle not;
> Feet have they, but they walk not;
> Neither speak they through their throat."

The final word in sarcasm concerning these false gods is found in one brief sentence:

> " Neither is there any breath in their mouths."

This comes in the poetic and remarkable passage in the prophecy of Isaiah, as to how men make gods. They take a tree and carve it, adorn it, decorate it, and set it up in its appointed place. Having done so, the prophet declares that where it is placed it will remain. It cannot move. If they leave, they must carry their gods with them. He places the God of Israel in contrast with all such as he shows that He is

a living God. Men make idols and carry them. God
makes men and carries them. It is upon that fundamental fact that the whole Christian superstructure is
erected. When at Cæsarea Philippi Christ asked that
earliest group of His disciples, Who do you say that
I am? the great confession of Peter was uttered in the
words:

" Thou art the Messiah, the Son of the living God."

The phrase occurs four times in the course of this
letter. Emerging in our text, it is found again in chapter nine, verse fourteen, in a declaration that the Son
through the eternal Spirit, offered Himself to God that
He might purge our consciences

" From dead works to serve the living God."

In chapter ten, verse thirty-one, in another solemn
warning the writer says:

" It is a fearful thing to fall into the hands of the
living God."

In the twelfth chapter and the twenty-second verse,
when once again comparing the economy of the Son
with that of Moses, the writer says:

" We are not come unto a mount that burned with
fire that might be touched . . . we are come unto
Mount Zion, and unto the city of the living God."

The fourfold occurrence of the phrase is in itself

arresting. First the warning word, " Lest we fall away
from the living God " ; then a revealing word, the Son
came to purge our consciences that we might serve
the living God; again a warning that there is a danger
of apostatizing, and falling into the hands of the living
God; and finally, a prediction of an ultimate glory and
victory in a reference to the city of the living God.

The peril, therefore, is that of falling away from
that living God. The word rendered " falling away "
is a strong word. It does not mean stumbling merely,
but refers to apostasy which is definite, deliberate
departure from God.

We may be inclined to say at once that surely that
cannot be done, and yet the whole force of the warning is a revelation of the fact that such apostasy is
possible. No one ever intends to apostatize. There
was an hour when Simon Peter said to Jesus:

" Though all shall forsake Thee, yet will not I " ;

and there is no reason to doubt his sincerity in the
declaration. Nevertheless he did forsake his Lord,
and that so positively as to deny Him with oaths and
curses. Such apostasy, however, is never a sudden
thing. There are multitudes of people today who have,
in this sense, apostatized. They would resent being
described as infidels, but the living God is not real to
them in any practical sense. They have departed from
Him, dismissed Him from the realm of consideration,
and perhaps while still professing intellectual conviction of His existence, live as though there were no God.

In the words that follow, the writer reveals the process leading to this disaster, in the words, " an evil heart of unbelief." The arresting and almost startling word in the phrase is the word " unbelief." To illustrate it, the writer goes back to the history of the people in the wilderness. It is well to remember in this connection how many perished in the wilderness. Of the adult population that were brought into the wilderness at the exodus, only two entered Canaan, and those, Joshua and Caleb. Moses himself was excluded.

The writer then shows that the reason for this was that of unbelief. To summarize his arguments, he says these people had the message, God's speech through Moses. They disobeyed through unbelief, and consequently their hearts became hardened. An examination of the passage in which the text occurs will show the differing terms that are used therein to describe the failure of the people; sin, unbelief, disobedience. These are synonymous terms. They heard the word, but proved their practical unbelief by disobedience; and the result was that they lost their sensitiveness to the Divine order. There are people in the world today who will say of certain attitudes and actions, " My conscience does not condemn me." That may be a terrible thing to say, revealing the fact that the conscience is hardened, has lost its true functioning power. Oftentimes, when conscience does not condemn us, we should condemn our conscience. Unbelief is not failure in intellectual apprehension. It is disobedience in the presence of the clear commands of God.

The whole process and result is revealed in the sentences that follow, wherein the writer warns us in the words:

"Lest any one of you be hardened by the deceitfulness of sin."

It is thus that those who have heard the speech of God may apostatize from the living God.

Such a condition is described as "evil," an "evil heart of unbelief." The Greek word there rendered "evil" means harmful, destructive. Unbelief, in the sense of disobedience to the revealed will of God, whether through Moses or the Son, is not only merely wrong, but completely destructive of life. These people had had the word of God through Moses. We have it through the Son. They, having received that word through Moses, and disobeying it, were excluded from rest. If they were excluded because of disobedience to the word of Moses, how much more shall we be excluded from rest if we are disobedient to the voice of the Son.

In the midst of this passage there is a word which our translators have arrestingly and helpfully spelled with a capital letter, the word "Today." It occurs in a quotation from a Psalm. It speaks of hope, and the possibility of recovery, even though there may have been failure. If for any reason we have been disobedient to the voice of the Son, and if the callousing process has begun, it is still called "Today." "Today" is God's day of love, God's day of grace, God's day of the possibility of pardon and renewal.

VI

THE SON—GREATER THAN JOSHUA

" For if Joshua had given them rest, he would not have spoken afterward of another day. There remaineth therefore a Sabbath rest for the people of God. For He that is entered into His rest hath Himself also rested from His works, as God did from His."
—HEBREWS iv. 8–10.

As we study the letter to the Hebrews we are conscious of the panorama of the history of the Hebrew people as background. The time when God spoke through angels is recognized, and the superiority of the Son to angels demonstrated. That covers the Book of Genesis, in which neither prophet nor priest nor king is found. Moving forward, the time when God spoke to the new nation, which was created for the blessing of the world, through Moses, was under review. The superiority of the Son to Moses is shown. That covers the historic movement from Exodus through Deuteronomy.

Now, still moving forward, we come to Joshua, and the period when the people of God entered the land under his leadership, a period of failure, not of Joshua, but of the people. Thus throughout, the writer of this letter is using history for the illustration of great principles, the history of the times when God spoke to men through angels, when He would speak through a nation, and therefore spoke to that nation through Moses.

52

Now we come to the period when He still spoke to the nation through Joshua. We may summarize so far by saying with regard to the history of the nation, that Moses had led them out of slavery, but could not lead them into the land of possession. The Son came to lead men out of slavery, and into the place of full realization. Now Joshua led them into the land of possession.

The opening words of the Book of Joshua are significant:

" Moses My servant is dead; now therefore arise."

Moses had rendered his service faithfully, and had passed on. The purpose of God must move forward, and the man was found. Joshua then led them in, but was not able to give them rest. This further movement in the historic background is employed to reveal the glory of the Son, Who not only leads out of slavery and into the place of possession, but is able to give perfect rest.

The Greek word used here for rest means quite literally to settle down, and it is found in classical Greek, used to describe colonization. That, of course, is exactly the meaning of the statement, that, whereas 'Joshua took them into the land, he was not successful ultimately in bringing them into a settled condition. He could not lead them so that they really entered into their possessions. The contrast is intended, and of course is self-evident that our Joshua confronting humanity, said, " Come unto Me, and I will give you rest." That is to say, He leads out of slavery into the land, and brings to the place of complete realization, which is rest.

Let us examine this by considering first the limitation of Joshua and the unattained Sabbath; and secondly, the victory of Jesus, and the realization of the Sabbath.

The story of Joshua is in itself a fascinating one. He was born in slavery in those bitter final years of Egyptian bondage. There he lived for forty years. Then the Exodus took place. When the boy was born into the midst of brutal oppression, his father and mother gave him a name. They called him Hoshea, which quite simply means Salvation. It was a sigh, may we not say a sob, and yet a song of faith and hope. Quite evidently he was born at about the time when Moses made his own attempt to deliver his people, and had to leave the country, because he had zeal without knowledge. For forty years Moses was lost to sight, and perhaps almost to memory; and then he appeared, and deliverance was wrought for the people. Joshua being then forty years of age, marched with the people from bondage into liberty. It is quite evident that he was a man of power and ability, for Moses quickly discovered him, and he became what we may describe as Moses' right-hand man. He was with him for the forty years in the wilderness, and he and Caleb were the only two of the adult population who came out of Egypt, eventually to enter the land.

It was revealed to Moses that this man was chosen of God to carry on the work when he should have laid it down. Then he changed his name, taking the name given to him at his birth, Hoshea, and certain of the letters of the Divine name, Yahweh, or Jehovah, and weaving them into one, called him Yehoshua, or Joshua.

This, then, is the man called of God to continue the leadership of the people in fulfilment of the Divine purpose. The words inscribed on Wesley's tablet in Westminster, " God buries His workmen but carries on His work," are of perpetual application. Moses was dead, but Joshua was raised up. He was a warrior, and from the standpoint of strategy and tactics, as military experts today will admit, he was characterized by remarkable skill. From the standpoint of the Divine purpose we see him raised of God to cleanse a land from a degraded and corrupted people, and to plant therein a people governed in righteousness. The surgery of the heavens is sometimes necessary to purify the putrefactions of earth.

He was more, however, than a warrior. He was a great administrator. Using our old English expression, we may say that he compiled the Domesday Book of the people.

As he entered upon his work we have the wonderful story of how he was confronted by One with a drawn sword, evidently a figure in human form, so definitely so that Joshua addressed Him, and asked Him:

" Art Thou for us, or for our adversaries? "

The answer was that the Person thus addressed was " Captain of the host of the Lord." Here, unquestionably, we have one of the Christophanies of the Old Testament. From that moment all the activity of

Joshua became in a very real sense a spiritual adventure.

The account of his success as a warrior and administrator is a very remarkable one, but nevertheless it is self-evident that he was unable to bring the people to the place of rest. The Book of Joshua is followed by the Book of Judges, throughout which the restlessness of the people is evident. The lowering of their moral conceptions prevented them finding rest. The story of that book may be summarized by repeating three words seven times over: disobedience, discipline, deliverance. God is seen ruling; the people disobeying, as a result being disciplined, and then delivered. It is a history of constant restlessness. Joshua could not give them rest.

Looking back at these facts, the writer of the letter to the Hebrews reveals the reason of this continued lack of rest. These people had heard the message of God, the good tidings that told of the possibility of rest. They knew, moreover, that the secret of rest was that of abiding under the government of God. Nevertheless they were persistently disobedient. In that connection the writer makes a significant declaration which reads in the text:

"They were not united by faith with them that heard."

The Revisers in the margin suggest an alternative reading:

"It was not united by faith with them that heard."

Unquestionably that more accurately conveys the sense of the passage. They heard the good tidings, but they did not unite it—the message thus heard—by faith with themselves. The good tidings proclaimed revealed the secrets of rest in the land and in the economy and Kingdom of God. They heard, and in all probability intellectually accepted, but they did not link it with conduct by the act of faith. Here, in passing, we may note that we have an interpretation of the real meaning of faith. It is more than an intellectual apprehension, including ever the principle of volition which conforms in conduct to the thing heard. That is where these people failed, and all the subsequent history of them was characterized by restlessness, because of this failure.

That survey of the background leads at once to a consideration of the foreground. That foreground is concerned with Jesus as the Son of God, and two things are revealed concerning Him; first, that of His personal victory; and secondly, that of His way of securing relative victory.

When the writer here declares:

"He that is entered into his rest hath himself also rested from his works, as God did from His,"

in the text these pronouns are all printed with small letters. As a matter of fact they should all be printed with capital letters, for the references throughout are to Christ or God. Christ has entered into rest, as God entered into rest. God entered into His rest as Genesis reveals, when His creative work was accomplished.

Jesus entered into His rest when His work of redemption was accomplished. That records His personal victory.

That personal victory has issued in relative victory, the rest into which He entered followed His sharing of the restlessness caused by sin. In the days of His flesh, passing through the porches of Bethesda, He had healed a man, and in defending His action against the criticism of the rulers, He had declared:

" My Father worketh even unto now, and I work."

This work was continued and consummated, and it consisted in the activity which made possible the leading of others into the place of rest.

This being so, the writer makes his appeal:

" Let us therefore give diligence to enter into that rest, that no man fall after the same example of disobedience " ;

and in that connection immediately makes the declaration that

" The Word of God is living, and active, and sharper than any two-edged sword, and piercing even to the dividing of soul and spirit, of both joints and marrow, and quick to discern the thoughts and intents of the heart."

This great statement we constantly employ as referring to the Bible, to the Word of God in that sense. That may be perfectly permissible, but the reference

of the writer was not first to the Bible, but to the Son
Who is the Word of God.   It is of Him he says:

> " The Word of God is living, and active, and sharper
> than any two-edged sword, and piercing."

That the reference is to the Person is proven by that
which immediately follows:

> " There is no creature that is not manifest in His
> sight; but all things are naked and open before the
> eyes of Him with Whom we have to do."

Completing the statement, then, in this way we have a
contrast between the speech of God through the Son
and everything which had preceded it.   The Word of
God is not a document merely, but a Person, living and
dealing with personality, distinguishing between mind
and spirit, and thus figuratively dividing between joints
and marrow, that is, points of articulation and essence
of being.   The Word then discerns the thoughts, that
is the conceptions, and the intentions as well as the
purposes of the heart:

> " There is no creature that is not manifest in His
> sight; but all things are naked and laid open before the
> eyes of Him with Whom we have to do."

In this way the Son deals with the causes of unrest
in human personality, and so deals with them that
perfect rest results, when His authority is completely
submitted to.   He enters into personality, distinguishing between spirit and mind, laying bare the deepest

desire and intention of life. If it be true that complexes are at the root of all restlessness, He disentangles them, and brings them into proper relationship. When Jesus, the Son of God, the living and eternal Word, deals with a man, He invades the whole region of his personality, separates, divides, disentangles, loosens up, brings into true inter-relationship, and so produces rest.

If Joshua could have given these people rest

" He would not have spoken . . . of another day."

That day has dawned. The Greater than Joshua has come. Once again the writer uses the word " Today," which here also our translators have helpfully rendered by printing with a capital letter. We are living in that day, and the Son, the living Word, is still saying, " Come unto Me, and I will give you rest."

Here, therefore, the continued history reveals the abiding superiority of the Son. He leads out; He leads in; He gives perfect rest.

VII

THE SON—GREATER AS PRIEST

"Having then a great High Priest, Who hath passed through the heavens, Jesus, the Son of God, let us hold fast our confession."
—HEBREWS iv. 14.

IN the background of our present consideration, the Hebrew people are seen as an established nation, a Theocracy. Moses had led them through the wilderness. Joshua was appointed to bring them into the land. The writer of the letter was looking then upon the nation, at the centre of which stood the Tabernacle. This was " the Tent of meeting," the " Tabernacle of witness." The phrase " Tent of meeting " refers to the fact that it was the place where God and man met together, where the King and His subjects had a point of contact. The phrase " The Tabernacle of witness " refers to the fact that it was the place where God spoke, the place from which the people received the Divine word, the Divine instruction. In the inner place of that Tent and Tabernacle stood the mercy seat, overshadowed by the outspread wings of the cherubim; and between those outspread wings shone the mystic light of the Shekinah glory. It was there at that centre of the national life that priesthood functioned.

The writer of this letter having shown the superiority

of the Son to the angels, the messengers of the past; to the servant faithful in His house; to Joshua, who had led the people in, but could not give them rest; now recognizing the fact of the national life, with the place of the King at the centre, dealt with priesthood. From this point in the letter to the tenth chapter that whole subject of priesthood is under consideration, and the argument is that of showing, not merely the superiority of the Son to Aaron and the Levitical order, but the fact that the complete fulfilment of the priestly purpose is found in the Son, and in the Son alone.

In the earlier part of the letter the writer had twice already alluded to the function of priesthood, but said little about it. In the second chapter, speaking of the superiority of the Son to angels, he said:

> " It behoved Him in all things to be made like unto His brethren, that He might be a merciful and faithful High Priest."

Again, at the commencement of the third chapter he said:

> " Consider the Apostle and High Priest of our confession, even Jesus."

We may profitably pause here to consider the idea of priesthood in itself. The world has been cursed with false conceptions as to the values and functions thereof. When we turn to the New Testament we find the word priest, and its cognate words, constantly recurring. The word priest in itself means a holy person, carrying the idea of separation, sacredness, or sanctity. There is no light on the subject of the function of the priest in the word, but it does reveal the character necessary to the fulfilment of function.

When we turn to the Old Testament the word rendered " priest " always means one who mediates. The word there, therefore, does describe a function. We may take these two words with their two suggestions, and put them together. As we do so, we find that the priest is a mediator, and must be holy. The priest has to do with a holy God, but he stands in the presence of that God representing those who, in themselves, are defiled.

Thus the life of the Hebrew people as a nation under the Divine government, centred round the place of the Divine Presence, which was absolutely holy, and in itself was made up of those who were excluded from that Presence on account of sin. Therefore the sacred function of Aaron, and the whole Levitical priesthood was that of approach to God as mediating between Him and the people. In the spiritual realization of the Theocracy through Christ the day had passed for that priesthood, and that because in the Son the Priest had been found absolutely fulfilling the two ideas, that first of holiness of character as a necessity for approach, and that further of a mediatorial right and power, able to deal with the necessities of sinning men.

Turning then to this subject, the writer employs the phrase:

" Having then a great High Priest."

In the Hebrew economy the name of the priest approaching was ever that of the High Priest. The writer of this letter, realizing the superiority of the Son in His Priesthood, introduces an adjective, " great."

This " great High Priest," he declared

> " Hath passed through the heavens, Jesus the Son of God,"

and urged those to whom he wrote in the words:

> " Let us hold fast our confession,"

by which he clearly meant that they were no longer to turn back to those divinely appointed methods which were illustrative and transient. Beyond the splendours of the robing of Aaron, beyond the glory of the ritual of the Tabernacle, beyond the suggestion of eternal values in rites and ceremonies, is Jesus the Son of God, as a Priest.

So important is this theme, that beginning here in the fourth chapter, the movements run on, as we have said, into chapter ten. We take now, then, three lines of meditation, the office of the Priesthood as revealed in the context; the qualifications for fulfilling the priestly office as here declared; and then the contrast between the persons of Aaron and Jesus.

In dealing with the subject of the office of the priesthood we find the writer employed a phrase full of infinite significance, " the throne of grace." In that phrase we have a revelation of God; the Throne necessarily speaking of authority, sovereignty; while grace unveils the deepest fact in the nature of God. John, in the course of his writings in one superlative sentence, declared, " God is love." We fall short of the mark when we speak of love as an attribute of God. Love is His very essence. Grace is love in action. Thus the Throne speaks of law, and grace speaks of love.

The value of that phrase being recognized, we may come to a true apprehension of the function of priesthood. In order to the appropriation of the activities of grace, there must be submission to the authority of the Throne. Therefore, in the case of sinning men there must be mediation. All the partial lights of the old economy and all the clear shining light of the new find their full radiance and interpretation in the Person of Jesus, the Son of God. The Priest, therefore, is one through Whom the outsider may be brought to the Throne, and have communion therewith.

It is a very arresting fact that the institution of the order of the priesthood in the Hebrew economy was an accommodation of God to the weakness of men. If we read the nineteenth chapter of Exodus, we find that before any word was said about an order of priests, the Divine intention for the whole nation was declared in these words:

" Ye shall be unto Me a kingdom of priests, and a holy nation."

That is, a Kingdom of intermediaries, holy in character. The reference is to the fact that that nation was intended to stand between God and the outside world, creating a way of access to Him. The nation never

rose to the realization of that intention. At the
moment of original declaration the people were afraid,
and as we continue our reading of that same nineteenth
chapter we find a change of tone in the message of
God, made necessary by the inability of the people to
rise to the high ideal. Out of that came the appointment of the order of priesthood. All this does not
invalidate the importance of the priestly function. It
rather emphasizes the necessity for it in the midst of
fallen human nature.

In that connection, proceeding, the writer declares
the functions of the priest when he says:

" That he may offer both gifts and sacrifices for
sins."

That is the whole meaning of priesthood. Sin which
excludes the God-made man from fellowship with the
God Who made him, and loves him, must be dealt with
in some way, in order that he may find his way back to
God. It is this function which is perfectly fulfilled in
Jesus, the Son of God.

Very beautiful, and full of infinite comfort for
sinning men are the qualifications of priesthood as
described. The priest must be one " who can bear
gently with the ignorant and erring." In these two
words two conditions are revealed. The ignorant are
those who do not know, and the erring are those who,
knowing, either wilfully or unwilfully wander from the
way.

The throne of law is the throne of grace. Around

the throne are those who are ignorant and erring. The priest who stands between such and God is to be one who deals gently with those so described. So sacred is the vocation that no man can choose to be a priest. He must be called of God, and anointed. It is so sacred a matter that the responsibility for the appointment of a priest must ever rest with God, and not with man.

We now look at the application of this in the contrast between Aaron and the Son of God. Aaron was called of God. Responsibility for his appointment rested upon God. As we look back, however, to the old economy, with Aaron thus appointed, we are reminded that as to approach, he first had to offer sacrifices for his own sin. Thus Aaron is seen, splendid, isolated, Divinely appointed, fulfilling in a remarkable way the ideal, but before he entered, he himself needed mediation, sacrifice, the offering for sins. Consequently, even though by Divine arrangement in grace, Aaron passed into the Holiest, there was something lacking in his priesthood, Divinely appointed as it was. In the case of Jesus, the Son of God, there was no such lack, and therein lay the ultimate superiority of His Priesthood over that of Aaron.

In applying this truth the writer employed psalms, the linking together of which, though widely separated in our arrangement of the Book of Psalms, is very arresting. He first quoted from the second Psalm, and declared that Jehovah said of One:

> " Thou art My Son,
> This day have I begotten Thee " ;

and in immediate connection he quoted from the one
hundred and tenth Psalm:

> " Thou art a Priest for ever
> After the order of Melchizedek."

Jesus, therefore, is a Priest upon the basis of His
Sonship, and of His appointment as King.

His fulfilment of the qualifications necessary to
perfect functioning are declared in the words with
which we are perfectly familiar and love so well.
Slightly changing the reading from the negative to the
positive form, the declaration is that He is

> " Touched with the feeling of our infirmities. . . .
> One that hath been in all points tempted like as we are,
> yet without sin."

The phrase rendered " yet without sin " is very full of
meaning. It indicates far more than that He did not
yield to temptation; declaring rather that He was in
Himself sinless.

The declaration that He was touched with the feel-
ing of our infirmities necessitates an understanding of
the word " infirmities." We are apt to use that word
in a false way, in application to failures that really are
sins. The real meaning of the word rendered " infirmities " may be expressed in the phrase, points of
weakness, or vulnerable points. In all these He was
tempted like as we are. This is revealed superlatively
in the story of His temptation in the wilderness. Man
is vulnerable in the matter of his spiritual life, and

relationship to God; in the realm of his physical life, and hunger for bread; in the realm of his aspiration and ambition, and his desire to possess kingdoms. The temptation of our Lord as recorded shows Him in each of these positions, but completely victorious over every attack. It is because He entered into these experiences so completely on the human level, that He is able to be gentle with the erring.

Then we find the stupendous declaration that because He had dealt with sin, He "passed through the heavens." A little later in the letter the writer speaks of Him, and says:

> "Such an High Priest . . . made higher than the heavens";

and still later he says of Him, He

> "Entered . . . into heaven itself, now to appear before the face of God for us."

He "passed through the heavens." He was "made higher than the heavens." He entered into the final heaven to appear as the great High Priest.

The value of all this for us is found first in the charge:

> "Let us hold fast our confession,"

which means, Let us not be deflected from our confidence in this Priest by any argument within our own soul, or by any suggestion that we need any other mediation.

Connected with this is the call, " Let us draw near."
There is nothing we need more constantly to remember
than the abiding necessity for priestly mediation when
we draw near to God.   We ever have to come to Him,
saying:

> " Nothing in my hands I bring,
> Simply to Thy Cross I cling."

Our High Priest is in the heavens.   Therefore, we may
ever draw near to God through Him.

VIII

THE SON AND THE OATH OF GOD

"God, being minded to show more abundantly unto the heirs of the promise the immutability of His counsel, interposed with an oath."
—HEBREWS vi. 17.

HAVING placed the Son against the background of Hebrew history to the point where the nation was seen as an established Theocracy around a system of worship and a mediating priesthood, the writer turned aside to a section in which he uttered words of almost dread solemnity, warning against the peril of apostasy, or the refusal of the speech of the Son.

The argument now goes back in the history of the Hebrew people to Abraham, and the writer returns there for a definite purpose. He returns to that point where God spoke through angels, and to the particular hour in which He made His final appearance to Abraham in connection with the offering of Isaac.

It is to be observed that the writer's quotation from the Genesis story is not complete, although sufficient for his purpose. If we return to the story itself, as recorded in Genesis (xxii. 14–19), we shall find that in that communion, God had said to Abraham:

" In thee shall all the nations of the earth be blessed."

The writer is drawing attention to the fact that when God said this, He said it on oath, the oath of God.

Now that is the arresting and perhaps amazing thing in this story. We find that God uses the language which reveals Him as putting Himself on oath:

" By Myself have I sworn, saith the Lord."

That which He asserted on oath was that His counsel is immutable, that it cannot be changed, that whatever the appearances of the hour may have been to Abraham, that whatever the passing of the years may have brought to the nation, the one thing that remained certain was that of the immutability of the Divine counsel. The application at the moment was to the declaration that He had made:

" I will bless thee . . . and thy seed . . . and in thee shall all the nations of the earth be blessed."

That was the counsel of God, and He put Himself on oath that it was immutable. I repeat, that it is at first sight an amazing story. This may be emphasized by the fact that our Lord, when uttering the great Manifesto of His Kingdom, forbade the taking of oaths, as He said:

" I say unto you, Swear not at all."

He declared that their Yea or Nay would be enough, by which, of course, He meant that they were to be such men that when they said Yea or Nay, they meant what they said. And yet God is here found putting Himself on oath.

It is important that we consider carefully the illustration which the writer of the letter to the Hebrews employs to illuminate the matter, for he is careful to point out exactly what he means. He says that when men swear, they "swear by the greater." That was the custom of the time, and it is the custom still. It still obtains in English courts of justice, where a man, sworn to give evidence, does so by taking an oath in the form of kissing the Book. In doing that he is swearing by something greater than himself. Now, says the writer, in every transaction and utterance the oath is final for confirmation, and by that he means the oath is the basis of confidence. If a man takes an oath by appealing to that which is higher than himself, it is supposed that what he shall utter shall be the truth, and that constitutes a basis of confidence. Now that is what the Genesis story tells us that God did, and this letter to the Hebrews reaffirms it. But at once we see the difference. A man taking an oath appeals to some one, or something higher than himself. This God cannot do, for there is none higher than Himself. Thus He took the human method, qualified by His own Being and nature, and His action was final for confirmation, that is, it became the basis of confidence for Abraham.

It may be said that there was no necessity for God to put Himself on oath because of what He was in Himself. We have another illustration of that, of which there are so many in the Biblical account of

God, of His accommodating Himself and His method to meet man in his need. The writer shows that when he uses the phrase, " being minded to show." Man needed some confirmation beyond the simplicity of the declaration. In his dealings with his fellow-man, the oath was the method by which this confirmation was gained. God in condescension came to that human level, and, adopting the human method, put Himself on oath.

The disparity between the oath of a man and the oath of God lends increased importance to the fact. A man's oath, if it be sincere, and acted upon, binds him to an outside authority. When I take the oath, I am recognizing that authority, and appealing to it, because I am obedient to it. The oath of God necessarily depended upon His own final and complete authority. Therefore He sware by Himself.

Having already referred to it, we now inquire more particularly what was this oath of God? It was a declaration of the immutability of His counsel. The word " counsel " there refers to volitional determination, leading to purposeful action; and that counsel was concerned with the blessing of Abraham and his seed; and, as the Genesis story reveals, the blessing of " all the nations of the earth."

Canon Farrar tells us of something to be found in Jewish literature, which is imaginative, but which is very suggestive. In the Treatise Berachoth, Moses is pictured as speaking to God about this oath, and as saying this:

" Hadst Thou sworn by heaven and earth, I should
have said they will perish, and therefore so may Thy
oath; but as Thou hast sworn by Thy great name, that
oath shall endure for ever."

If this be imaginative, it nevertheless does reveal the
confidence created by this action of God. There can
be no doubt that faithful souls, through centuries, had
built upon that oath of God. God had given to them
not merely the declaration of His intention, but had
condescended to employ the method of man, and had
sworn by Himself that that intention should be carried
out.

Now the writer of the letter to the Hebrews, conscious of the confidence thus placed in that oath of
God, is showing how it had literally and completely
been fulfilled in the Son of God. The intervening centuries had run their course, and now he speaks of
Jesus, and shows how through Him the oath is ratified
and fulfilled. In writing to the Galatians, Paul spoke
of the seed of Abraham, and declared, " Which is
Christ " ; and a little later he said:

" If ye are Christ's, then are ye Abraham's seed."

He was then writing, not to Hebrews, but to Gentile
Christians. The Hebrew people after the flesh, had
been excommunicated by the word of Jesus spoken in
Jerusalem:

" The Kingdom of God shall be taken away from
you, and shall be given to a nation bringing forth the
fruits thereof."

Thus the counsel of God is immutable. His purpose
cannot change. His word to Abraham:

> " I will bless thee . . . and thy seed; and in thee
> shall all the nations of the earth be blessed,"

has come to the point of actual and historic fulfilment.
Christ is the Seed fulfilling the covenant, and those
who are Christ's are " Abraham's seed."

Now we may glance at what the writer has to say
about Jesus in this connection. He declared that He
has entered

> " Within the veil . . . as a Forerunner, having
> become a High Priest for ever after the order of
> Melchizedek."

This fact constitutes the " anchor of the soul," the
ultimate secret of confidence. The oath of God,
fulfilled in the Person of His Son, as He passes into
the heavens, assures the heart.

An arresting word in this connection is the word
" Forerunner." It marks a difference between Christ's
passing within the veil, and everything that had preceded it in the ritual of the Hebrew people. Aaron
had entered within the veil once a year, but never as a
forerunner. He entered as the representative of those
who were left outside. But they were always left outside. No one followed Aaron when he entered within
the veil to stand in the presence of the ark and the
mercy-seat. When Jesus passed within the veil, He
went as a Forerunner, which at once suggested that the

way was open for others to follow Him. He was the Seed in which, and through which, all nations were to be blessed; and He had made it possible for all those who were His to pass with Him into the same place. That surely was the symbolic suggestiveness of the rending of the veil when He died.

Another matter which is suggestive is the use the writer makes of a figure of speech in this connection. He speaks of " an anchor of the soul." Now an anchor has been from time immemorial a symbol of hope. It is found so employed in Greek literature. It was also suggestive of safety in danger. We drop the anchor, and the ship is moored; and because of that, we realize safety from peril. Nevertheless, let it be remembered, that an anchor, as a matter of fact, prevents a ship functioning according to its capacity. No ship is fulfilling the true meaning of its being when it lies at anchor. As Kipling shows in his sketch, " The Ship that found herself," she does that, not when riding at anchor, but when moving out into the deep. We remember there was a time when Paul and others with him, having flung the freight overboard, and the tackling of the ship, let go four anchors, and prayed and waited for the day. It is self-evident that while the ship was thus held, she was not fulfilling the meaning of her existence. Now the remarkable thing is here that the writer uses that figure in such a sense that it breaks down, and yet fulfils itself. The anchor is cast within the veil, that is, it is flung out into the vastness of the eternities, not to the shoals near the shore, but into the deep itself. Thus the figure of speech fulfils its intention as it emphasizes anew the immutability of the counsel of God. This counsel found its fulfilment when He passed within the veil; and into all the vastness of that which lies beyond, the anchor is cast. The confidence of the soul is ratified because One has passed within the veil, the Forerunner, leaving the way open for us.

Through angel ministry God had dealt with men, and in this meeting with the father of the nation He met human frailty with an oath. The oath, or the declaration made on oath, became personal by Incarnation, and that Incarnation led to the Cross, and through it to resurrection and ascension wherein the Son of God passed within the veil. That, then, is the secret of our confidence. Nearly a hundred years ago Edward Mote wrote a hymn which catches up and gloriously expresses the teaching which we have been considering. The refrain of that hymn is found in the words:

> " On Christ, the solid Rock, I stand,
>   All other ground is sinking sand."

Three of the stanzas, in each case ending with the refrain, run thus:

> " My hope is built on nothing less
>   Than Jesus' blood and righteousness;
>   I dare not trust the sweetest frame,
>   But wholly lean on Jesus' name.
>
> When darkness veils His lovely face,
>   I rest on His unchanging grace;
>   In every high and stormy gale,
>   My anchor holds within the veil.

His oath, His covenant, His blood,
Support me in the whelming flood;
When all around my soul gives way,
He then is all my hope and stay."

IX

THE SON—AFTER THE ORDER OF MELCHIZEDEK

" It is witnessed of Him,
Thou art a Priest for ever
After the order of Melchizedek."
—HEBREWS vii. 17.

IN our previous study we saw the greatness of the Son manifested in that He ratified the oath which God uttered to Abraham when He, the Son, passed within the veil as a Forerunner.

All the symbolism is that of the Hebrew nation, religion, and worship. The function of one standing within the veil is necessarily that of priesthood. To this subject the writer of this letter returned at this point. Aaron had passed within the veil on the great day of Atonement through the running years. Within, he acted as a priest, and having fulfilled his function, passed out again. Jesus entered within the veil to remain, but as He did so, the veil was rent in twain, thus leaving the way open for others to enter in.

The function of the priesthood of the Son, having thus passed within the veil, is then suggested by the declaration:

" It is witnessed of Him,
Thou art a Priest for ever
After the order of Melchizedek."

Thrice already the writer had made reference to this fact. In chapter five, and verses five and six, we find these words:

> " So Christ also glorified not Himself to be made
>   a High Priest, but He that spake unto Him,
>   Thou art My Son,
>   This day have I begotten Thee:
> as He saith also in another place,
>   Thou art a Priest for ever
>   After the order of Melchizedek."

Again, in the tenth verse we read:

> " Named of God a High Priest after the order of Melchizedek."

And once more, in chapter six and verse twenty, we have the statement:

> " Whither as a Forerunner Jesus entered for us, having become a High Priest for ever after the order of Melchizedek."

In the first reference two quotations were brought together from two widely separated Psalms as to their place in the Psalter, and very likely as to the time of their writing. Linking them, he applied them to the Son of God. From Psalm two he quoted:

> " Thou art My Son,
>   This day have I begotten Thee."

From Psalm one hundred and ten he quoted:

> " Thou art a Priest for ever
> After the order of Melchizedek."

Thus the Person referred to is the Son, and His office as Priest is described as being after the order of Melchizedek.

The whole priesthood of the Hebrew people had been Levitical, of the order of Aaron. Jesus was not of the tribe of Levi, but after the flesh of the tribe of Judah. He was not, therefore, a Priest of the Aaronic order; but as the writer says in this most arresting declaration, He was " a Priest after the order of Melchizedek."

Necessarily that raises an inquiry and commands attention. What do we know of Melchizedek? We find that his name occurs only twice in the whole of the Old Testament literature. Here in this letter it occurs nine times. In the Old Testament we find the historic account of him in Genesis, which takes us back two thousand years before Christ. From that moment on, no further reference is made to him in the history of the Hebrew people, and neither is any reference made to him in the prophetic literature. A thousand years after the historic event recorded, David names him in one of his Psalms. It was a Psalm concerning the Messiah, and while thus looking on to His advent, David referred to the historic incident, and says of the coming One:

> " Thou art a Priest for ever
> After the order of Melchizedek."

All this is arresting and suggestive. Something took place, the record of which we are given. A thousand years passed, and a singer referred to this event. Another thousand years passed, and the One appeared to Whom reference was made. And then the writer of this letter quotes from the Psalm, and thus referred to the history.

We go back, then, first to the historic account. The name is in itself arresting. Melchizedek, Malkiy-Tsedeq, King of Right. In his reference the writer of the letter to the Hebrews is careful to say:

" Being first by interpretation King of righteousness, and then also, King of Salem."

There has been much discussion as to the location of Salem, notwithstanding the fact that the writer of the letter adds the significant words, " Which is King of peace " ; thus showing that no city was referred to.

We are told two things about this Person in history; first, that He bore a name which signified that He was King of righteousness, and, secondly, that because He was King of righteousness, He was also King of peace. Thus suddenly in the history of Abraham this Person appeared, Who is described as a Priest of El-Elyon, that is, of the Most High. We are not told whence He came or where He went after this appearance to Abraham. The appearance occurred at a remarkable moment. Abraham had parted company with Lot, who had chosen for himself the well-watered plain, while Abraham remained a pilgrim under the terebinths of

Mamre, in the company of God. When the compromis-
ing Lot was in trouble, the faithful Abraham went to
his help, and overcame the opposing kings, recovering
the spoil. To Abraham in the hour of victory this
Melchizedek appeared. We observe with care the
priestly function He exercised. It is significant that
nothing is said about the offering of sacrifices. He did
not come with burnt-offerings, or anything which suggested sacrificial approach. He came bearing bread
and wine for the refreshment of the weary servant of
God. Moreover, He blessed him, and still exercising
the priestly function, He blessed God, that is, He
offered worship to Him. Then He received tithes, and
His doing so indicated His superiority to the one who
brought them.

There are many interpretations of this story which
of course demand respect. In its simplicity it is
remarkable, in that there appeared to Abraham a man
unknown and unplaced, the writer saying of Him:

"Without father, without mother, without genealogy."

Thus, for His action He had no authority vested in
human ancestry, and His action was not committed to
posterity.

Amid the varying interpretations to which I have
referred, I would now say that I am personally convinced that this is the story of a Christophany; that
here, as upon other occasions, there was granted to a
man the appearing and ministry of none other than the

Son of God, the One Who is King of righteousness, and therefore King of peace.

A thousand years after the event David wrote:

> " Jehovah saith unto My sovereign Lord,
>   Thou art a Priest for ever
>   After the order of Melchizedek."

Thus David had gone back to the historic story, and declared that the ultimate Priest should be One like Melchizedek, without father, without mother, without genealogy. It is certainly an arresting fact that this was the Psalm which our Lord made use of when He was attempting to bring the rulers of His time to a recognition that the Messiah would be the Son of God. The rulers in their reply to the Lord's question showed that they were familiar with their Scriptures, as they immediately replied that Messiah should be the Son of David; and our Lord challenged them at once as to how He could be David's Son, and David's Lord. They evidently did not grasp the significance of the quotation and question. We, however, see distinctly that after the flesh He was the Son of David, but in essential Being He was the Son of God. Therefore His Priesthood was after the order of Melchizedek.

The Son entered within the veil as a Forerunner, and there He abides, exercising His priestly function. Thus all the mystic qualities revealed in the historic account of Melchizedek came to their ultimate fulfilment in Jesus. When we attempt to account for Him wholly within the human, we fail to understand either

His Person, or the meaning and power of His Priesthood.

The purpose of the writer, therefore, was that of
showing the difference between the Priesthood of the
Son and every other. Those referred to were divinely
ordained, divinely instituted; but in themselves they
could not meet human need. Such need is completely
met in the Priesthood of the Son.

As the matter is considered we find that in this
Priesthood there was fulfilled not only the mystic suggestiveness of the historic Melchizedek, but also the
fulfilment of the principles revealed. As the writer
says, "First King of Righteousness." The One Who
represents us within the veil, in the power of an endless
life, is not exercising a Priesthood which for one
moment lowers the standards of morality; being first,
always first, King of righteousness. Any presentation
of the mediatorial work of our Lord, and His consequent saving power, which suggests that there is any
lowering of the standard of righteousness, is false.

It is because He is King of righteousness that He is
also King of peace. The eternal order is first pure,
then peaceable. This Priest within the veil has entered,
having made provision by which human sin can be
dealt with both as to its pollution and its paralysis;
and in and through Him man may stand in the presence
of the Holiest.

Later in this seventh chapter the writer summarizes
the whole matter. Because the Son is a Priest after
the order of Melchizedek, One Whose Personality
transcends all human measurements and limitations,

One Who stands first for righteousness, and so secures peace:

> " He is able to save to the uttermost them that draw near unto God through Him."

That word " uttermost " is a great word. It has within it two qualities, which merge into a complete revelation, the two qualities are represented by *panteles*, which means all, and is a word of quantity; and *telos*, which is a word of reach, and means extent. He is able to save to the uttermost, that is in Him there is fullness of provision in quantity, and fullness of provision in duration.

Thus the word " salvation," with which we are so familiar, is seen in all its fullness and glory. The teaching of the New Testament shows that it has its tenses, so that we may say, looking back, we were saved; and thinking of the present, we can say, we are being saved; and lifting our eyes and looking on, we can say:

> " Now is our salvation nearer than when we believed."

We were saved. We are being saved. We are going to be saved. He is able, because of the mystery of His eternal Personality, His fidelity to righteousness as a basic principle; and His Cross by which He made peace; to save to the uttermost.

The priesthood of Aaron was a wonderful priesthood, Divinely ordained, but it for ever fell short, even in its highest exercise, of meeting human requirement.

Its value was that it foreshadowed the possibility of the meeting of that requirement. The Priesthood of the Son of God does more than shadow forth a possibility; it creates an experience.

This Priesthood, moreover, is one which continues to bring forth bread and wine, all that is needed for the restoration and sustenance of such as are workers together with God, as Abraham was in the dim past. In that old story we read that when the king of Sodom offered gifts to Abraham, he replied:

> " I will not take a thread nor a shoe latchet . . .
> lest thou shouldest say, I have made Abram rich."

This is ever the attitude of those who receive all the ministrations of the Priest, Who is the Son of God. They find in God through Him both their shield and their exceeding great reward.

X

THE SON—THE BETTER COVENANT

" He is the Mediator of a better covenant, which hath been enacted upon better promises."—HEBREWS viii. 6b.

WE now reach the point where the writer of this letter commences to show the superiority of relationships, resulting from the superiority of the Person of the Son. In dealing with this subject it will be found that these relationships are described as better; a better hope, better covenant, better promises, better sacrifices; and indeed the word runs on in harmony with its first occurrence, when the writer spoke of the Son as " better than the angels," and occurs in the letter altogether thirteen times. Whereas the old economy, though Divinely appointed, was now superseded by a new economy, it was every way better than the old.

Our present meditation has to do with the better covenant enacted upon better promises. All God's speech to the Hebrew people in the past had been based upon the covenant He had made with them, when He brought them unto Himself. Whether He had spoken through Moses, Joshua, the priesthood, prophets, seers, or psalmists, everything had been the

89

carrying out of the covenant made between Him and His people.

The writer, therefore, now proceeded to show that the speech of God to man in its finality through the Son is also conditioned by a covenant, but it is a new covenant and a better one. Necessarily this does not for a moment make any reflection on the old covenant on the Godward side, as to its grace, or on the man-ward side as to its demand.

As we have proceeded in these studies we have kept in mind throughout the history of the Hebrew people, for the letter was written to Hebrews. At this point, then, the writer turned back and quoted from the prophecy of Jeremiah. God has spoken through angels, Moses, Joshua, Aaron, and the prophets. The reference to Jeremiah is to a day in the history of the people when everything seemed to have failed. There was the glory of the beginning when angels talked with men, from God; when Moses was the Divine spokes-man. Now a quotation is made with length and full-ness from a period in the history, of the most disas-trous failure. Jeremiah was in many ways the most tragic and heroic of all the prophets. He was the spokesman of God to the nation for forty years, during which, still uttering the Divine Word, there were no immediate moral or spiritual results achieved. In the work of prophesying for God there are moments in the case of all His messengers when it does seem as though nothing was being accomplished. In all the long line of the messengers of God to men, it is doubt-ful whether we have the record of any who knew that experience more constantly and overwhelmingly than Jeremiah. For forty years he spoke, and the only result he received was ribaldry and persecution, and persistence in the ways of iniquity. Israel had already gone into captivity, and Jeremiah conducted his ministry during the last forty years in the history of Judah. At the beginning he shrank from the work to which he was called, and so heroically carried out.

It was during that dark period that he looked on through the gloom and saw the dawning of a day, and he spoke of it as of a day when God would make a new covenant with men. Now the writer of this letter to the Hebrews, long centuries after Jeremiah had uttered his prophecy, declares that its fulfilment is found through the Son.

The value of the argument is discovered in a consideration of the contrast between the covenants. Looking back to the old covenant, on the basis of which God had spoken, the writer quotes from this prophet, predicting a new covenant, which was to be better than the old.

As we have seen in a previous meditation, the old covenant was based upon promises God made on oath. The promises referred to were first the word spoken to Abraham, as the father and founder of a race, " I will bless thee " ; and secondly, the resulting words, " All nations shall be blessed in thee." In these words we have a revelation of God's side of the covenant. Necessarily to a covenant there are two sides, and the fulfilment on either side must be contingent upon fulfilment by the other side. When it is affirmed that

God must keep His covenant with the Hebrew people this is often forgotten. If one of the parties to a covenant fail to fulfil their obligation, the covenant is thereby disannulled. On the part of God, therefore, we see that the covenant was made upon the basis of the promise that He would bless the nation in the interest of all the nations. If we return to the account in Exodus of the making of that covenant, we find these words:

"If ye will obey My voice indeed, and keep My covenant, then ye shall be a peculiar treasure unto Me from among all peoples: for all the earth is Mine."

Thus the human responsibility in the covenant was that of hearing and obeying the voice of God. The law was given to them, inclusively in the Decalogue, and in interpretative applications in the whole Mosaic economy. The history proves how completely they had broken down. It is one of persistent failure. This is discovered in the records. God has ever had His elect remnant of loyal souls, but from the standpoint of the nation as a whole, with which the covenant was made, they had failed from first to last. First they clamoured for a king, and God gave them what they clamoured for, that they might learn their folly. The final fact in their failure was, of course, the appalling one that they killed the Son of God. But let it be carefully remembered that before they did so, He with full authority had excommunicated them from the position to which they had been appointed. He did so in the words:

" The Kingdom of God shall be taken away from you, and shall be given to a nation bringing forth the fruits thereof."

Thus we have a covenant made, a covenant broken on the human side. The writer of this letter declares plainly that had that covenant not broken down, there would have been no new covenant. Jeremiah from the distance, with prophetic vision, saw that even then God could not fail, and that, therefore, there must be, and would be, a new covenant, a better one, which would produce ultimately the fulfilment of the Divine intention. Let us hear the prophetic word concerning this new covenant, in its fullness.

> " This is the covenant that I will make with
>   the house of Israel . . .
> I will put My laws into their minds,
> And on their heart also will I write them;
> And I will be to them a God,
> And they shall be to Me a people;
> And they shall not teach every man his
>   fellow-citizen,
> And every man his brother, saying, Know
>   the Lord;
> For all shall know Me,
> From the least to the greatest of them.
> For I will be merciful to their iniquities,
> And their sins will I remember no more."

In the closing part of that quotation we have a revelation of the basis upon which the promises are made. The final words reveal the deepest fact:

> " For I will be merciful to their iniquities,
> And their sins will I remember no more."

Those immediately preceding show the immediate result:

> " For all shall know Me,
>   From the least to the greatest of them."

All the promises preceded these closing statements, and result from the facts declared in them; that is to say that the new covenant begins with the moral cleansing of those who enter into it in fellowship with God.

That, of course, is the central fact of Christianity. All the New Testament teaches it. The voice of Jesus attested it as being the very purpose of His coming. In the annunciation to Joseph the angel had declared it:

> " Thou shalt call His name JESUS: for it is He that shall save His people from their sins."

There was nothing of that nature found in the old covenant. Now relationship with God on the part of man is made possible by this cleansing of the nature from sin. The result of this cleansing is the knowledge of God, which is infinitely more than knowledge concerning Him.

The result of all this is found in the contrast between the issues of the new covenant, and the experience of the old. In this new covenant the law of God is to be inward and spiritual. As to the old it was external. Its moral requirement is in no sense an abrogation of that included in the covenant of old. The Ten Commandments stand for ever as a revelation of law; but now these requirements are to be written on the heart, the seat of the affections, and on the mind, the centre of intellectual apprehension. To repeat, the law is now inward and spiritual, resulting from the mediatorial work of the Son, Who cleanses the moral nature, and brings us into such relationship with God that His will is made known to us directly and individually.

This is still further emphasized in the declaration that under the new covenant:

"They shall not teach every man his fellow-citizen."

In fellowship with God, every man will know the will of God. This truth was emphasized by John in his first letter:

"And as for you, the anointing which ye received of Him abideth with you, and ye need not that any one teach you" (ii. 27).

Thus the new covenant means that in the last analysis we need seek guidance from none other than the indwelling Spirit, Who abiding within us, as the result of the cleansing of the nature, makes known the will of God.

The whole difference, then, between the old covenant which is also Divine, and the new which is Divine and final, is the difference between the letter and the spirit. Paul, writing to the Corinthians, referring to this matter said:

"A new covenant, not of the letter, but of the spirit;
for the letter killeth, but the spirit giveth life" (2 Cor.
iii. 6).

It is a remarkable fact that the "letter" appeals to
humanity in a strange way. Men love rules and regu-
lations. They feel it is easy to obey rules. Now the
whole history of man proves that it is not so. The
law as it was given by Moses was the law of the letter,
and the difficulty of obedience was revealed in all the
traditional explanations that had been contrived by
men in the passing centuries. It is a most arresting
fact that our Lord in His teaching poured contempt
upon these traditions, and constantly showed their failure, saying indeed that men had substituted them for
the commandments of God. Therefore, the covenant
of the letter is neither easy nor safe.

On the other hand, the law of the "spirit" seems
insecure and difficult. As a matter of ultimate experience, it is the only law that is at once easy and safe.
When the life of man is brought into personal, living,
first-hand relationship with God, it is not difficult
either to discover the will of God, or to obey it. Of
course these things are impossible until there is the
complete surrender to the Son, which results in the
cleansing of the life. In the cultivation of our fellowship with God, through the One to Whom we are thus
submitted, and by Whom we are cleansed, we are
enabled to fulfil our obligation in the covenant.

When we consider this matter seriously and carefully, we are necessarily conscious of our own oft-
times breakdown and failure; but we also know that

such failure is due to disobedience on our part at some point. If we would know all the fullness of the blessing brought to us within this covenant, we must see to it that we give all diligence to seek that immediate guidance of the Spirit, which is possible to us; and as we find it, to yield immedi..: obedience thereto.

XI

THE SON—THE BETTER WORSHIP

" For Christ entered not into a holy place made with hands, like in pattern to the true: but into heaven itself, now to appear before the face of God for us."—HEBREWS ix. 24.

HAVING considered the superiority of the new covenant, the writer now turned to the subject of the superiority of the worship that is made possible to men through the Son. Once in this chapter we find the word " worshipper " (ix. 9). It is found again in the plural number in the second verse of chapter ten. These are the only places where the word occurs, but the cognate verb occurs in this chapter nine, at verse fourteen, where it is rendered " serve." This is an arresting fact, showing the relationship between worship and service. It will be remembered that in the hour of our Lord's temptation, He said to the enemy:

" It is written, Thou shalt worship the Lord thy God, and Him only shalt thou serve."

Worship, in the last analysis, is the secret of service, and service is an expression of worship.

The first thought of worship is that of rendering homage and adoration in the presence of God, whether by an individual soul, or by a company of men and women united in the sacred activity. The outcome of such worship is ever that of service. At this point, however, we are principally concerned with worship as adoration.

In our examination of this letter we have seen that the background has ever been that of the Hebrew people, their history and their ritual. This is still so, and in order to bring into clear relief the beauty of worship as made possible through Jesus Christ, the writer goes back to the worship of the Hebrew people; and it is good for us, therefore, to recall the background of the ritual of the Tabernacle, its worship and its service, in order to see the more clearly the foreground of the heavenly Tabernacle, its worship and its service.

In looking at the background, it is important to remember that the writer did not go to the Temple, but to the Tabernacle itself. This is in itself significant. Writing as he certainly did, before Jerusalem had been surrounded by enemies, and the Temple had been razed, the actual background was that of Herod's Temple which took sixty years to build. His references, however, were not to that Temple, neither were they to Solomon's Temple, the full description of which is found in the Old Testament. There is no doubt that the Tabernacle was the true pattern received from God, and the Temple was an accommodation to human weakness, just as the priesthood had been, and also kingship. We glance back, therefore, to the Tabernacle in relation to the encampment of Israel. The tribes are seen ranged round the central place of worship. Between them and the actual Tabernacle were

the outer courts. To these the writer made no reference. Centring observation upon the Tabernacle itself,
he points out that there were two parts to it, the outer,
known as the Holy Place, and the inner as the Holy
of Holies. In the outer place, which is the vestibule
of the actual centre of worship, he draws attention to
a candlestick, or lampstand, having opposite to it a
table with the shewbread upon it. This was according
to the pattern given in the mount. Here the word
" the pattern " refers to the model of something
already in existence. He says, therefore, that this
Tabernacle was a representation in the material realm
of spiritual facts. Under that dispensation God was
teaching through pictures. In the Holy Place was the
lampstand, symbolizing the office of the nation; and
opposite to it the table of shewbread, symbolizing
man's fellowship with God.

Before the veil was found an altar of incense. The
reading of this passage may suggest that this altar was
inside the veil; but let it be carefully noticed that the
writer says, " having an altar of incense," which
emphasizes that as the way of approach. A reference
to Exodus will show its true place. There were senses
in which it belonged to the inner realm, but it was the
last thing outside. Actually behind the veil there was
nothing but the ark, which was a chest of acacia wood,
covered by what is described as " a mercy seat," literally, " a propitiatory," this being overshadowed by
two cherubim, the highest symbolism of created life.
In the old economy, shining there on the mercy-seat,
under the outspread wings, and beneath the watching

eyes of the cherubim, a mystic light was shining, which was called the Shekinah, and was the symbol of the presence of God. It was to this Tabernacle that the writer went for his illustration. Had he gone to Herod's Temple, he would have found no ark. When Pompey sacked the Temple, looking into the Holiest place, he declared there was nothing there.

We have seen what was there in the Tabernacle. Thus the whole picture is that of a nation surrounding a place of worship, which is the very heart and centre of its life, the place of its highest activity, worship in the presence of God. As we look back at the old Tabernacle, none is found within that Holy of Holies for 364 days in every year. The people were camped outside, and were represented by priests, who continually, every day passed into the Holy Place, attending to the lamps, which symbolized witness, and to the shewbread, which was the symbol of communion. Once in the year, on the great day of Atonement, one man entered the Holy of Holies. He passed in alone, carrying with him fire and blood. First he took the blood that spoke of his own necessity for cleansing, and then that which represented those who were outside. At sunset he left the Holy Place, and there it remained in splendid and awful isolation for another 364 days. As we look at the picture we see the masses of the people outside as they are represented by this one man. Not one of these people had a conscience that had been cleansed. The need for the cleansing of the conscience had been emphasized, and the fact that man can only enter the

presence of God and render Him acceptable worship
by some mystery of sacrifice, which provided for
cleansing.

Now against that background comes the great
declaration:

> " Christ entered not into a holy place made with
> hands, like . . . to the true." He " entered into heaven
> itself, now to appear before the face of God for us."

That " now " has eternal value, and not a transient
one. The true place of worship is heaven itself. To
say that is to recognize a difficulty in any conception
we have at present of location. To think of the universe is to make it necessary to believe in some region
where there is the supreme manifestation of God. I
do not say where God is, for He is in all heavens. The
centre of all worship is therefore in the presence of
God, in that place, however we may conceive of it,
which is the place of His supreme manifestation. Now
the writer says that the Son entered " heaven itself."
We remember how, in the account of His ascension,
it is said that Jesus led His disciples out, and lifting
up His hands in blessing, was parted from them, and
they saw Him pass out of sight into the heavens. The
heavens received Him. In the declaration of the writer
here the word is used in the singular number. He
passed " into heaven itself." That is the true place
of worship. If when we gather in any building we do
not find our way into that spiritual region, our worship
fails.

Moreover, when the Son entered into heaven itself,

He entered to remain there. Ere entering He had
" offered Himself," the reference being to the mystery
of Calvary, as the tenth chapter shows, when it refers
to " the offering of the body of Jesus Christ once
for all."

He Who thus had offered Himself, passed into
heaven, " to appear before the face of God for us."
This, in itself, is an arresting declaration, especially
when compared with the story we have in Exodus
(chap. xxxiii.). Moses desired to see God, and was
told:

> " Thou canst not see My face, for man shall not see
> Me and live."

He was allowed only to look upon His back. Now
the Son passed into heaven to appear before the face
of God, and that on our behalf. Thus the ultimate in
worship is made possible through the Son's offering
of Himself, and consequent appearing before the face
of God.

Thus we may gather up the values of the teaching
of the letter at this point. The true place of the worship of man is not in an earthly building. Such build-
ings are indeed sacred, but they are vestibules, con-
veniences on the material level, built for the gathering
together of men and women; in order that such may
transcend their locality, and find their way into heaven
itself.

In the last analysis, the Tabernacle, with all its symbolic construction, spoke of exclusion. Men were not
allowed to enter into the place where the Shekinah

glory shone. Only one could enter, and he might not
tarry there. The veil spoke for evermore of exclusion.
When Jesus died, the veil of the Temple was rent in
twain from the top to the bottom, a symbolic and
supernatural action, revealing the fact that the way
was now open into the very presence of God for all
those who come through the One Who has entered in
all the authority of His final priesthood. The fore-
shadowing of this possibility was given by our Lord
Himself, not to a Jew, and not to a priest, but to a
Samaritan, and to a woman withal. To her He had
said:

> " The hour cometh, when neither in this mountain,
> nor in Jerusalem, shall ye worship the Father. . . .
> The hour cometh, and now is, when the true worship-
> pers shall worship the Father in spirit and truth."

It was the realization of this tremendous spiritual
fact which inspired the writer of the hymn, which says:

> " Heaven comes down our souls to greet,
>   While glory crowns the mercy-seat."

Thus we can worship in the home, in the church building, or wherever we are. These earthly localities are
not final places of worship, but they are places where
we may enter into the presence of God, and, doing so,
find the Son of God appearing " before the face of God
for us." The highest, holiest worship, then, is the worship offered through Him in that immediate Presence.

XII

THE SON—PRIVILEGES AND RESPONSIBILITIES

" Having, therefore, brethren, boldness to enter into the holy place by the blood of Jesus, by the way which He dedicated for us, a new and living way, through the veil, that is to say, His flesh; and having a great Priest over the House of God; let us draw near with a true heart in fulness of faith, having our hearts sprinkled from an evil conscience, and our body washed with pure water; let us hold fast the confession of our hope that it waver not; for He is faithful that promised; and let us consider one another to provoke unto love and good works; not forsaking the assembling of ourselves together, as the custom of some is, but exhorting one another; and so much the more, as ye see the day drawing nigh."—HEBREWS x. 19–25.

FOR our present meditation the whole of this paragraph is needed, revealing as it does privileges and responsibilities, resulting from the fact of the finality of the speech of God to men through His Son.

It is well to remember that the letter to the Hebrews is not intended to interpret the speech of the Son, but to insist upon its authority. In our previous studies we have considered the Son as superior to angels, to Moses, to Joshua, to Aaron. We have also considered the fact that upon that superiority of personality and function through the Son, there is established for men a new covenant written upon the heart, and based upon personal first-hand fellowship with God. The result of this creation of a better covenant is that of the establishment of a better system of worship. We have a right of entry, not into an earthly tabernacle, but through the earthly into the heavenly, into the Holy of Holies, so that we may worship God, without any other mediation than that of the one great Priest.

It is at that point in the letter where the paragraph now under consideration commences. All these things being so as to privilege, responsibility inevitably results. As we have seen before in the course of the letter, the writer again and again turns aside to utter words of solemn exhortation and warning. The full passage here begins at verse nineteen, and ends at verse thirty-seven; and the latter part of it is characterized by warnings. With these we are not dealing now, but with the section revealing the responsibilities devolving upon us, on account of our high and holy privilege through Christ Jesus our Lord.

The recognition of privilege is seen in the repetition of the word " Having " twice over, and that of responsibility in the repetition of the words " Let us " three times. In this way let us consider the matter, beginning then with the privileges referred to.

In considering these, we assume familiarity with the stately arguments concerning the Son, which we have been considering, and to which we have now made reference. We have seen Him superior to angels in the fact of His Sonship; superior to Moses in the fact that He is Son and Master of the House; superior to Joshua in that He leads His people into rest; superior to Aaron in that His Priesthood is for ever after the order of Melchizedek. We have seen the new centre of worship established, and the possibility of approach upon the basis of a new spiritual covenant.

Now the writer makes no reference to Moses, to Joshua, to Aaron, but to that great fact of our access to the Holiest through the mediation and priesthood of our Lord. " Having, therefore, brethren, boldness to enter in." That is the first " having," and it refers to our right of access to God, based upon all the things that have been said concerning the Son of God. The place is referred to, and under the symbolism of the Tabernacle, that place is the Holy of Holies, beyond the veil, wherein in the old economy was found the ark with the mercy-seat, and the overshadowing cherubim, and the shining of the Shekinah glory. Our privilege is that of passing within that veil.

We are reminded also of the way of our entrance:

" By the blood of Jesus . . . through the veil, that is to say, His flesh."

The value of that expression, " His flesh," is exactly that found in the prologue to the Gospel of John, when he, writing of our Lord, said, " The Word was made flesh." Our right of entrance is through that, but it must be carefully borne in mind it is through the rending of the veil; and our right, therefore, to enter this place of worship is not created by the Incarnation, not because God has been manifest in flesh, but by that of the death and resurrection of the incarnate One.

The writer, continuing, describes this as " a new and living way." With that phrase I pause for a moment, because the Greek word rendered "new" there, literally means newly-slain, and the phrase accurately translated reads, "a newly-slain and living way." In this connection we may call to mind the fact that in the Apocalypse, John speaks of beholding:

> "In the midst of the Throne . . . a Lamb standing, as though it had been slain."

This is our way into the Holy of Holies, and we have no other right of entry there. Man, by reason of sin, has forfeited his right of fellowship with God, and that right is restored through the Priest.

The whole great truth finds simple expression in Mrs. Alexander's wonderful hymn written for children, but which in many ways sets forth this truth more perfectly than any other has done:

> "There is a green hill far away,
>   Without a city wall,
> Where the dear Lord was crucified,
>   Who died to save us all.
>
> There was no other good enough,
>   To pay the price of sin,
> He only could unlock the gate
>   Of heaven and let us in."

And this He did by the rending of the veil of His flesh, that is by the mystery of His atoning death. Here we stand, face to face with the fundamental truth concerning our right of access to God, and perhaps it finds expression in another children's hymn, full of simple beauty:

But though we're sinners every one
    Jesus died!
And though our crown of peace was gone,
    Jesus died!
We may be cleansed from every stain,
We may be crowned with bliss again,
And in the land of pleasure reign,
    For Jesus died! "

In considering this first " having," we pause for a moment with another technicality of translation. The word rendered " boldness " means, quite literally, boldness of speech. We find it in the Acts of the Apostles, when it is said of Peter and those with him, that their boldness of speech arrested and astonished the Sanhedrin.

It is boldness of speech that we have in the Holy of Holies, which means that there we find freedom of utterance in the presence of God. It is a great and almost overwhelming statement and thought, that in that Holy Place we are able to stand, and talk face to face with God. Kipling, in his introduction to one of his books, referring to men that he knew and honoured, described them as " gentlemen unafraid." That phrase exactly describes our privilege.

And yet we pause, because the majesty of God is necessarily so overwhelming that it is difficult to understand how the thing is possible until we come, as we now do, to the second " having."

" Having a great Priest over the House of God."

And here for the moment the emphatic word is that

word "over," which means that our Priest is there in full and final authority; and we stand there not merely admitted through His work, but in fellowship with Him.

The lines of another hymn occur to me in this connection:

> " So near, so very near to God,
>   We cannot nearer be;
> For in the Person of His Son,
>   We are as near as He.
>
> So dear, so very dear to God,
>   We cannot dearer be,
> For in the Person of His Son,
>   We are as dear as He."

These, then, are the great privileges referred to.

In view of these privileges the writer points out the responsibilities resulting. Let us first set them out in order, each being introduced by the phrase, " Let us."

> " Let us draw near."
> " Let us hold fast."
> " Let us consider one another."

An examination of these three phrases will show that the form of the verb in each case suggests not so much an act as continuity. " Let us draw near " means continuously. " Let us hold fast " means persistently. " Let us consider one another " means constantly.

Observe again, " Let us draw near . . . in fullness of faith." " Let us hold fast the confession of our hope." " Let us consider one another to provoke unto love." Three words stand out: faith, hope, and love. In the ·first two, responsibility is strictly individual, although the pronoun is in the plural. In the third case the application is social, embodying the fact of fellowship.

Taking these in separation, we begin with the first. We are to draw near. We know that the way has been opened for us. We have the right of access to the Holy of Holies. Our responsibility is that we avail ourselves of this privilege. Privilege is only powerful as it is practised. Through Christ the great hour has come in which no longer in Jerusalem or Gerizim, but wherever the human soul is, the way is open. It is not enough to know this. We must enter. Moreover, we are to do so " in fullness of faith," and faith is the faith that is fixed upon the Priest and His mighty redeeming work. As we approach, we are not to waver in doubt, for the everlasting mercy of the Father is seen in the glory shining upon the mercy-seat. It is important that we recognize that before going, therefore, into this place of worship there must be a place of preparation by confession, and the seeking of the putting away of whatever defilement we may have contracted. Granted these things, however, we may come, through our Priest, into the presence of God with freedom of utterance, with all boldness of speech.

Our responsibility, moreover, is that we come, holding " fast the confession of hope." We may express this hope whereby we are saved as being the onward expectation and desire for the full realization of all wrought for us in and through the redeeming work of our Lord:

> " Every one that hath this hope set on Him, purifieth himself, even as He is pure."

Our hope, therefore, including as it does the ultimate in the processes of the ages, is immediate confidence in the ultimate, complete, full realization of the Divine purpose. Faith and hope are ever joined together. We are to draw near, then, holding fast the confession of our hope. The ground of our confidence in this is contained in the pregnant sentence, " He is faithful that promised."

> " My hope is built on nothing less
> Than Jesus' blood and righteousness."

Our hope is never built upon ourselves, or upon our own endeavours. It is created by the certainty that He will not fail. Hope is radiant. Hope is buoyant. Hope sings its song on the darkest day. Hope chants its anthem on the roughest way. Thus we are to come, daringly, in fullness of faith; and joyously, holding fast the confession of our hope.

But once more. There can be nothing finally self-centred in Christian experience. When experience tends to self-confidence, it is perishing. Therefore, the writer says, " Let us consider one another." Therein lies a great principle as to responsibility. Men and women who really know God, and know what it is to stand in His presence, cannot be careless concerning each other. The writer expresses this responsibility by saying we are to "provoke unto love and good works." That in itself is an arresting method of speech. It seems at first that there is something contradictory between the word "provoke" and the word "love." An examination of the word "provoke" rather adds to this sense, because the Greek word is the one from which we derive our word paroxysm; and it is interesting that in our common use of it we usually apply it in the sense which finds expression in the phrase, a paroxysm of rage. It is the word that was used to describe Paul's emotional upheaval in Athens, when, seeing the city full of idols, his spirit was provoked within him. Now the writer speaks of a provocation that is kindled by love. Our love is no merely soft, piquant sense. It is in itself a fire which consumes, and it is to be exercised on behalf of others.

Continuing, he shows how this is to be done, and first says:

"Not forsaking the assembling of ourselves together, as the custom of some is, but exhorting one another."

That is to say, all the privileges which are ours individually we are to share with others. At the end of the Old Testament literature we find a message in which Malachi, referring to days of decadence, declares that there remained a remnant of souls of whom he said:

"They that feared the Lord spake one with another."

That was the practice of fellowship. Concerning those he wrote:

"The Lord hearkened and heard,"

which is a very arresting declaration when the Hebrew words are rightly apprehended. The first one, "The Lord hearkened," is a word which literally describes the pricking of the ears with quick action, described by that phrase, which shows a sensitiveness and an attention which is marked. The prophet dared to say that that is what God does when His people are talking together. The second word, "heard," while still referring to the same idea, has another emphasis, for it means to bend over, listening attentively.

Thus our responsibility as we enter in is a social one. We come with a sense of inter-relationship.

This meditation may be very simply summarized by the repetition of words which fell from the lips of our Lord in the upper room, in His final intimate conversations with His disciples. He uttered them in connection with the symbolic act of washing their feet. He said to them:

"If ye know these things, happy are ye if ye do them."

This is what the writer of this letter is showing. The whole paragraph marks the relationship between knowing and doing. Privileges perceived and not practised become paralysis. Having the right of entry, having the fellowship of the Priest, let us respond, and fulfil our responsibilities. Life is to be mastered by faith, and not by doubt; it is to be for evermore illuminated by hope, and not darkened by despair; and in its activity love is to be practised in fellowship. These are the privileges of the Holy Place; and unless we fulfil our responsibilities, we cannot enter into all the values of these privileges.

XIII

THE WITNESSES OF THE PAST TO FAITH

"Therefore let us also, seeing we are compassed about with so great a cloud of witnesses, lay aside every weight, and the sin which doth so easily beset us, and let us run with patience the race that is set before us."—HEBREWS xii. 1.

THE last three chapters of the letter to the Hebrews are of the nature of appeal on the basis of all the arguments that have been advanced. The subject of these chapters is in a very special way that of faith, faith in God, and therefore faith as the supreme need of human life. Thus in the final movement the underlying philosophy of life comes into clear revelation.

In the opening sentences of the letter the writer, declaring that God had spoken to man, divided the ages into two parts—first, that in which He had spoken to the fathers through prophets, and secondly, that in which He has spoken in His Son. The whole argument has been that of showing the superiority of the messages of the Son, and how that word of God is final.

The purpose of the speech of God to men, whether in times past, or through the Son, is that men may exercise faith in Him. Whether He spoke through angels, through leaders—Moses, Joshua, priests or prophets, or whether He spoke through the Son, His

one purpose has ever been that men may find Him,
and finding Him, repose their confidence in Him.

The whole account of revelation is that of God's
approach to man, in order thus to inspire man's confidence in Himself. That is why, having thus massed
the arguments which prove the superiority of the
speech of the Son, and the finality of that speech so
far as God's revelation is concerned, in this final movement the writer addresses himself to this great subject
of faith.

Whereas I have spoken of the last three chapters,
the whole section begins at the close of chapter ten,
where the writer quotes from the Hebrew Scriptures:

" My righteous one shall live by his faith,"

or as it may be rendered, and has been rendered:

" The just shall live by faith."

It is well to remember at once that this was God's
answer to one of His own messengers, Habakkuk, one
of those prophets through whom He had spoken to
His people. Moreover, it was the word of God when
he was confronted with difficulty as he looked upon
the circumstances in the midst of which he was living.
So perplexed was he that for the moment he was an
agnostic as to the government of God. Looking out
on things as he saw them, Habakkuk said in effect,
Why does not God do something? It was then that
God said to him that He was doing something, but
that if He told His servant what, he would not believe

Him. Nevertheless He did tell him what He was doing, He was girding Cyrus. This raised a greater
perplexity in the mind of the prophet, for he could
not understand how God could make use of such a
man as Cyrus. It was then that God gave him the
secret of all life in the great declaration:

" My righteous one shall live by faith."

Coming then to the close of the letter, making his
great appeal, the writer quotes these central words.

In reading them we usually put the emphasis on the
word " just " or " righteous," and there is a sense in
which that is correct. Nevertheless there are senses
in which the emphasis should be on " live." That is
to say, it declares that life, in all the fullness of the
term, is maintained by faith. Or to state it from the
other side, the ultimate result of faith is full-orbed life.

In the eleventh chapter, so full of romance, the
writer surveys the human history from the Biblical
standpoint, giving illustrations of the power of faith,
and showing its constant triumph. Thus he leads up
to the appeal of the first verse of chapter twelve. It
is of the utmost importance that we should carefully
consider the meaning of this appeal. Perhaps I may
illustrate by saying that in my boyhood's days I often
heard sermons on this text, which were very interesting, but not based upon true interpretation. The idea
was that the writer was looking upon our Christian
life as a race, the goal of which is heaven, and that
those already having reached heaven, were watching

us in our running. That was the explanation of the phrase " Seeing we are compassed about with so great a cloud of witnesses." As a matter of fact, that is not all the meaning of the appeal. These people referred to as a cloud of witnesses are not described as watching us at all, but as speaking to us, witnessing to us. I am not now arguing as to whether or no those who have gone before see those of us who remain. I think as Bishop Bickersteth has suggested in his matchless poem, " Yesterday, Today, and Forever," under certain circumstances they may be permitted to see and visit us. Leaving that subject, however, and fastening our attention upon the actual meaning of the writer, it is as we have said, that all their life witnesses to us concerning ours.

Now let us in the briefest way look over the cloud of witnesses as referred to, all of them speaking to us of the value and power of faith in God. Having done that, we shall be able to give attention to the appeal made.

The reference to the power of faith opens with a remarkable declaration which indeed is a cosmic one. The writer declares that the elders by their faith had witness borne to them. It was through their faith that they received whatever revelation they did receive from God. He then declares that by faith also " we understand that the worlds have been framed." I cannot refrain from saying that that ever seems to me an unfortunate translation. The word the writer employed was the Greek word which means ages. As at the opening of the letter he declared that through

the Son God had fashioned the ages, so now he affirms that we understand through faith that the ages
have been thus framed by the word of God. This fact
is indicated in the margin of the Revised Version. In
our thinking today we look back and speak of ages
under mineral figures, the Stone Age, the Copper Age,
the Iron Age, and also the Golden Age. This writer
declares that such ages have been and are under the
government of God, and that through faith we understand this. It cannot be proved in any other way.
This necessarily means, as the writer declares further,
that things which are seen have not been made out of
things which do appear. By faith we grasp the reality
behind the manifestation. By faith we understand
that behind phenomena there are noumena.

Then leaving these cosmic declarations, human history is seen, and it is interesting to notice that the
writer selects his illustrations from all the methods
wherein God had spoken to man in the past, Angels;
Leaders, Moses, Joshua; the Priests, and the Prophets.
His speech through angels covers the period from Abel
to Joseph, and the illustrations given are those of
faith reposed in God, because of such messages. Abel
worshipped, Enoch walked, Noah walked and worked;
and all these by faith in God.

Then passing to the Hebrew history, he commences
with the one outstanding figure of Abraham, and
shows how all his life and action were based upon faith
in God. He obeyed as he turned his back upon an
ancient civilization; presently he offered his son; and
finally he obtained the promises, not their fulfilment,

but the certainty of their fulfilment. Thus in him, difficulty is transmuted into triumph by faith in God. The references to Isaac, Jacob, and Joseph present them all as men looking into the future, and uttering words of confidence concerning that future.

Coming to the leaders, he refers first to the faith of the parents of Moses, who was hid three months by them. Then the faith of Moses himself, who made his great choice at a critical moment in his life thereby. Through all his ministry he continued by faith, " as seeing Him Who is invisible."

In the case of Joshua, it was by faith that the walls of Jericho fell down. At this point occurs that reference which must have been startling to a Hebrew reader, but nevertheless does show the principle of faith at work. I refer to the reference to the harlot Rahab.

It was here that the writer, recognizing the vastness of his theme, says that the time would fail him to tell of " Gideon, Barak, Samson, Jephthah." This is not a chronological sequence, but a collection of outstanding personalities, four of them being judges, one a king, David, and then finally the greatest of the judges, Samuel. Finally in a phrase, " the prophets," reference is made to the whole of that period of revelation.

Passing from his reference to these personalities, he speaks of the deeds accomplished by faith:

> " Subdued kingdoms, wrought righteousness, obtained promises, stopped the mouths of lions, quenched the

power of fire, escaped the edge of the sword, from
weakness were made strong, waxed mighty in war,
turned to flight armies of aliens."

And then in a minor, plaintive word:

" Women received their dead by a resurrection."

Following on, the deeds were revealed to be accomplished by endurance in which the men and women of
faith oftentimes were found hiding in dens and caves
of the earth, concerning whom the writer in a parenthesis indites a fitting memorial to all such:

" Of whom the world was not worthy."

In the whole of this illustrative passage we see the
principle of faith at work, that faith which is the substance, the underlying reality of all things.

Then comes the marvellous conclusion:

" These all, having had witness borne to them
through their faith, received not the promise, God having provided some better thing concerning us, that apart
from us they should not be made perfect."

Some little while ago Dr. Simpson preached a sermon on the words, " And all flesh shall see the glory
of the Lord together." In that sermon he distinctly
showed how that the full glory of the Lord will only
be revealed when men see it together. We are march-
ing towards that goal. We are carrying on where our
fathers left off. The goal is that of the city of God

built. The race therefore that we are called upon to run is towards that ultimate in human history, wherein will come the answer to the prayer we so constantly pray, as He taught us:

> " Thy Kingdom come, Thy will be done on earth, as it is in heaven."

That is the race that is set before us.

The appeal, then, is found in the text, and its force is discovered by the repetition of the phrase twice over, " Let us," " let us." In the first section of it we are charged:

> " Let us lay aside every weight, and the sin which doth so easily beset us " ;

and in the second:

> " Let us run with patience the race that is set before us."

The first appeal has to do with the preliminaries, and the second with the ultimate.

In dealing with the matters which we have described as preliminaries, we are told what we are to lay aside in order to the fulfilment of the ultimate. The writer speaks of " weights," and " the sin which doth so easily beset us." The question may naturally arise as to what are the weights we are to lay aside; and the answer may be given inclusively and simply by stating that weights are the things that hinder our running the race. It is well for us to remember that we cannot

tabulate these weights for other people. Something
that may hinder me in running may not hinder my
brother; and something which hinders him, may not
hinder me. I venture to name one weight only, and
it is the weight of trying to find out what my brother's
weight is! A censorious criticism of my brother may
hinder me in my devotion to the race. Indeed, too
often we are hindered by endeavouring to remove the
mote from the eye of another, while a beam is in our
own. Peter was guilty of this very thing when on the
shores of Tiberias, looking at John, he said to Jesus,
"What shall this man do?" and it is well to remember
that our Lord immediately told him, to put it quite
bluntly, to mind his own business:

> "If I will that he tarry till I come, what is that to
> thee? Follow thou Me."

Moreover we are to lay aside "the sin which doth
so easily beset us." Perhaps there is no verse with
which we are more familiar in the New Testament,
and at the same time one which is so liable to a false
interpretation. It is quite arresting to notice that our
Revisers have suggested in the margin that we should
read, "the sin which is admired of many." I do not
hesitate to say that that is not translation, but it is
true interpretation. The Greek word employed by the
writer of this letter is the word *euperistaton*. If we
take this word to pieces we find it simply means, the
sin in good-standing around. Perhaps it may be admitted that that is not easy of interpretation. It has
been suggested that it refers to some garment that

hinders running. The Revisers, however, have suggested that it is a much admired sin, and I believe have here reached the true intention. The sin of refusing to believe is not in evil standing, but rather in good standing. There are some people who seem to imagine that intellectuality demands a mixture of cynical unbelief. Let all that be as it may, the one fact abides as true, that such unbelief ever paralyzes the nerve of effort. Unbelief in God invariably issues in unbelief in man, and therefore unbelief in the future. That easily besetting sin is to be laid aside.

In conclusion let it be emphasized that the text for this meditation is incomplete. A glance at the Revised Version will show that it ends with a comma, and the words immediately following are necessary to final interpretation:

> "Looking unto Jesus the Author and Finisher of faith, Who for the joy that was set before Him endured the Cross, despising the shame, and hath sat down at the right hand of the throne of God."

To that we come, all being well, in our next meditation.

To summarize then for the moment, we see that those named were witnesses to the power of faith; and moreover, that with rare exceptions, they failed; nevertheless, because of faith made their contribution to the ultimate purpose of God.

Moreover, as we pass over the chapter we are met by surprises. We are surprised by the absence of some names. This of course must not be over-emphasized, as the writer does not profess to name all; but at least it is worthy of careful thought that in that succession, no priest is named. We are surprised also by some names that are included: Samson, Jephthah, Rahab.

The chapter, however, includes them all, and says that, while they witnessed to us of the power of faith, they did not reach the goal, and we are thus called upon to continue in the course toward that goal, which must eventually be reached.

XIV

THE ONE WITNESS

" Looking unto Jesus, the Author and Finisher of our faith, Who for the joy that was set before Him endured the Cross, despising shame, and hath sat down at the right hand of the throne of God."
—HEBREWS xii. 2.

IN our previous meditation we were considering the first verse of this chapter, a verse in which the writer was looking back over the line of history from Abel, with its illustrations of men and women who lived by faith. It is indeed a marvellous roll of heroes and heroines of the world history. The world was not conscious of their greatness. The writer in a parenthesis said concerning them, " Of whom the world was not worthy." Nevertheless they lived and wrought and suffered and triumphed by faith.

In the light of that history, those to whom the letter was addressed, were urged to continue in the great succession, " Therefore let us also." The appeal is that we do not permit the past to be violated by our action,

> " Seeing we are compassed about with so great a cloud of witnesses,"

that is, those who bear witness to us of the value of faith. We are called upon to lay aside the weights and the sin admired of many, and run the race. That

is the great appeal. It is, as we have said, that we
carry on, that we do not let the enterprise of God in
the world down, that we set our faces towards the same
goal, and run on the same principle, and with the same
diligence.

We now come to words which are closely linked to
those already considered. There is a sense in which
the previous meditation was in itself unfinished. The
appeal of the witnesses is made, but there is something
more to be said, and that something is final.

The first word of this verse shows the intimate connection between what is now to be said, and what has
already been said. It is the word " looking," a parti-
ciple marking continuity.

The whole burden of the writer of this letter has
been concerned with the supremacy and authority of
the Son of God. Without for a moment departing
from that conception, in these words he places Him
on a level with ordinary human life. It is significant
that here he makes use of the human name, " Looking
unto Jesus." It is true that he does that again and
again in the course of the letter; but there is a significance in its use here. Glancing back over chapter
eleven, we read names: Abel, Enoch, Noah, Abraham,
Isaac, Jacob, Moses, and others, and at last JESUS.
He is in the same line, in the same succession, the same
humanity, and the same race. By a transcending act
of literary inspiration, he says in effect, The Son of
God Who is supreme and final, lived His life on the
same level, and by the same principle that men are
ever called to live.

I think the reader of this verse in his Greek New Testament would inevitably be arrested by this first word, " Looking." It places no such arrest upon the mind of the English reader, which I think is the fault of translation. Weymouth, in his rendering, has given due weight to the Greek word, as he has it, " Looking off unto Jesus." If we are reading the New Testament in all the stories of Jesus, and those in the Acts, and indeed in the letters, we constantly necessarily find the writers making reference to the use of the eyes; and in our English language, as in the Greek, different words are employed to signify the differing use of the eyes. In the Greek there is a word which simply means looking in the ordinary sense. There is yet another which means to look with perception, with understanding. There is another which implies earnestly inspecting as we look. There is yet another which means to watch critically. These are but illustrations, which might be multiplied. All this to emphasize the fact that in the word employed here by the writer of this letter, we have one that has never before occurred in the New Testament, and is never again found. It has as its root significance, a looking which can only be described as that of staring; not a casual glance, not the looking of complete apprehension, not the look of investigation, not the look of critical activity, but the look that suggests amazement, the seeing of something which has completely captured the mind. Here, however, that root is strengthened by a prefix *apo*, which suggests not merely the staring with wide-open eyes, but such complete capture by

the thing seen that all other visions have faded. We
are to look off. The supreme value of it is gathered
by a contrast between it, and what has already been
said. We are to see the witnesses, but there is another
vision which will turn off our eyes even from them,
and from all other matters. The word suggests first
the element of surprise, and secondly, that of such
complete capture as to make one unmindful of all else.

That, then, is the real secret of running this great
race. The witnesses are of value. They argue mag-
nificently for the strength of faith, but the final capture
of personality in order to continuity is not intellectual,
or shall I rather say, it is supremely emotional, but
is surcharged with the intellectual. By this word,
then, that the writer uses, is suggested that there is a
vision of Jesus which, once seen, will capture the soul,
and make it forget all else; and in itself, shall I say,
automatically loosen the hold of the runner upon the
weights that hinder, and make impossible the sin of
unbelief.

What, then, is this vision of Jesus? This inquiry
is answered in the statement of the writer. Continuing, he says, " Who," and by the use of this word
links all to be said with the One to Whom reference
has been made by His name " Jesus."

> " Who for the joy that was set before Him endured
> the Cross, despising shame, and hath sat down at the
> right hand of the throne of God."

In those verses we have a vision of our Lord in the
realm and region of His human life limned for us in a

few brief sentences, every one of them flaming with glory, radiant with light. We may first summarize by saying the writer presents to us the picture of an ideal life. He was the Author and Vindicator of faith; then shows Him as mastered by a passion for the victory of God, "the joy that was set before Him," but further reveals His procedure upon the pathway. "He endured the Cross, despising the shame"; and finally He is presented in His absolute victory, He "sat down at the right hand of the throne of God."

We may summarize in yet another way. Looking off unto Jesus, what do we see? A principle mastering life, faith; a passion inspiring and energizing life, the joy that was set before Him; a procedure in answer to the principle, and in obedience to the passion, enduring the Cross; a preëminence resulting from a principle and passion, and procedure, He sat down at the right hand of the throne of God. Let us glance at these things briefly.

First we see faith as a master principle. In order to understand the reference, we must pause with certain technicalities. The Revised Version reads:

"Looking unto Jesus, the Author and Perfecter of our faith."

We observe that the word "our" is italicized, and its introduction interferes with the true thought. The writer was not referring to the fact that He is the Author and Perfecter of our faith, in the sense of being the Originator and Completer thereof. That is all true, but it is not what is here stated. Again, against the word " Author," a marginal reading is suggested, " Captain." I do not hesitate to say that that alteration does not at all help us. The Greek word employed there, rendered into plain English, is File Leader. Now a file leader is one who goes first in the procession, the one who takes preëminence. The survey of the past began with Abel, and here reaches Jesus. The writer, however, declares that whereas historically at this point He was the last as to His relation to faith, He takes precedence over all that have gone before. He is the supreme Illustration in human life of what faith means, and of what faith does.

Once more, the word " Perfecter " would be better rendered as to its intention here by the word " Vindicator." Thus our Lord is presented not merely as the full and final interpretation of the value of faith, but the One Who in His own life and work has vindicated faith completely. Thus in the midst of the travail of the centuries, and of the men and women who have lived by faith in God, One Who appears takes preëminence as Revealer. He is the File Leader and the Vindicator of faith. If our faith is waxing weak, and our feet are growing weary, and we are not running as we should in the race, we are called upon to behold this superlative Vision.

As we glance back at the story of Jesus as told by the four evangelists, nothing is more remarkable, nothing is more arresting, nothing more persistently self-evident than the fact that He lived by faith. His faith was first of all faith in God; therefore it was faith in man; and finally it was faith in the future.

His constant fellowship with God, and His unceasing obedience to the will of God are the unanswerable proofs of His faith in God. Was He acting? What My Father gives Me, that I do. Was He teaching? I do not speak from Myself; what My Father gives Me, that I say. In this sense He was the File Leader of all in human history who have believed in God.

His faith in man is equally evident. His persistent belief in human possibility in spite of all its sin and degradation, stands out in an amazing way upon the page that tells the story of His life and service. When He came into the presence of a human soul, however derelict that soul might be, He came as One believing in the possibility of its recovery. Necessarily the ultimate thing to be said in this connection is that whatever others may think of human nature, He thought it worth dying for.

Once more, as we watch Him and listen to Him, we see His unqualified faith in the future. If we consider His ethical teaching, or His mystical teaching, His teaching of His own company, or His address to the crowds, we never find the faintest suggestion of His anticipation of ultimate failure. He fought to win. He suffered to save. He died to live. It was He Who did not

> " Bate a jote of heart or hope,
> But moved right onward."

In every respect the contrast between Him in this

matter of faith and all that had gone before, puts Him
at infinite distance.   Abraham's faith was wonderful,
but he lied.   Noah's was remarkable, but he sadly
failed.   This is true of all those referred to by the
writer.   But here is One Who never failed.   If I need
inspiration for my faith in running, I will see the
witnesses in passing, and then I will fix my eyes upon
Him, " looking off unto Jesus."

If that was the principle of His life, its passion is
perfectly expressed in the phrase, " the joy that was
set before Him."   We sadly miss the ultimate value
of the declaration if we think of the joy set before Him
as that of His return to the glory that He had laid
aside.   That was not the joy that filled the heart of
Jesus.   That was not the passion that sustained Him.
That was not the secret of His ability to say to His
disciples while yet in a tempest-tossed world:

> " My peace I give unto you . . . that My joy may
> be in you."

What, then, was His joy?   In answer to that we are
reminded of the prophetic word:

> " I delight to do Thy will, O My God."

His personal joy was ever that of doing that will.   All
His ethical ideals were interpretations of that will.   The
passion of His heart was to bring men into submission
to that will.   His prayers sought it, as did that which
He taught us to pray:

> " Thy Kingdom come, Thy will be done."

Through all the mists and the gloom that lay along the valleys, through the unfathomable darkness of His Cross, He ever saw the dawning of the day when God's will should be done on earth as in heaven. That was the joy set before Him. Because He ever beheld that as the ultimate, He always laid the measurement of the eternal upon the temporal, weighed the things of earth in the balances of heaven; and the joy that sustained Him was the certainty that one day the goal would be reached. To Him it was supremely true, to employ the apostolic words, " He rejoiced in hope of the glory of God."

If, then, the principle was faith, and the passion was the joy of the vision of full accomplishment, we inquire how, in view of these things, did He act? The answer is found in the declaration:

" He endured the Cross, despising the shame."

In reverent silence we meditate that matter. It was inevitable in a world where there was no admiration for the will of God, in seeking to know the will of God, rebellion against the will of God when it was known, that He must pass along the pathway of suffering. The writer speaks of enduring the Cross, and just beyond the text, employing the word again he says:

" Consider Him that hath endured such gainsaying of sinners."

Our old Versions read, " gainsaying of sinners against Himself." The Revisers read, " Against themselves."

Perhaps it should be said in passing that the American Revisers have restored the Authorized rendering. The difference is due to difference in MSS. Perhaps in the presence of this fact no one dares to be dogmatic. Nevertheless the whole spirit of the argument seems to need the interpretation of the Revised rendering. He did not endure the gainsaying of sinners against Himself. To the daughters of Jerusalem, who were following and lamenting His Cross, He said:

> "Daughters of Jerusalem, weep not for Me, but weep for yourselves, and for your children."

It is true that the men of His time were gainsaying Him, but what He saw was the tragedy of such gainsaying as it reacted upon the people themselves. That indeed is the very heart of the Cross. We notice carefully that, whereas in the eyes of men, the shame of the Cross was its terror, that He despised.

Here, then, we have the supreme inspiration for the running of the race, and the goal of it all was in His case that He sat down at the right hand of the throne of God. No language can be more perfect in setting forth the ultimate realization than this.

XV

THE GREAT APPEAL

" See that ye refuse not Him that speaketh. For if they escaped not, when they refused him that warned them on earth, much more shall not we escape, who turn away from Him that warneth from heaven."—HEBREWS xii. 25.

THE words, " See that ye refuse not Him that speaketh " reveal the ultimate purpose for which this letter was written.

The Hebrew Christians to whom it was addressed were in danger of falling away from faith, and the danger which thus threatened them was the result of intellectual wavering as to the full and final authority of Christ. That intellectual wavering, moreover, resulted largely from the fact that they had not put Christ completely to the test. They were Christians. They were believers. They had turned from the Hebrew form of religion to its ultimate fulfilment in Jesus Christ, but they were unstable. They were remembering the majesty of the old economy with its angelic ministration, and its guidance through Moses and Joshua and Aaron. They were undoubtedly somewhat confused by the apparent simplicity that was in Christ. The Temple was gone. The ritual had passed. All the splendour with which they had been familiar was no more. They were in danger of apostasy from the faith as they looked back, but did not sufficiently consider the fact of the Lord Himself. As we have already said, they had not put Him completely to the test, as the writer of the letter said:

> " Ye have not yet resisted unto blood, striving against sin."

They had been treating the whole matter largely on an intellectual level, and had been unable to grasp the full significance of Christ, because they had not yielded to Him a complete devotion.

It is well to remind ourselves at this point that these two points always go together. All intellectual wavering in the presence of Jesus Christ on the part of those who have known Him, is the result of a failure somewhere to carry out logically the things professed. The great idea was expressed by our Lord Himself in the words:

> " If any man willeth to do His will, he shall know of the teaching, whether it be of God."

The test of the Divine nature of the Christian message is that of " willing " to put it to the test. He whose life is yielded actively to the claims of Christ, even unto resisting unto blood if necessary, will discover that the teaching is of God.

This has been the line of the argument of the letter from beginning to end. In our first meditation we saw that it was a writing intended to set forth the full and final authority of our Lord by an interpretation of His

Person, and that in the speech of the Son we have
received the last thing that God has to say to man. It
may very easily be said that this speech of God to men
took place by the measurement of our calendars,
nineteen hundred years ago; and the question may be
asked, Is it so that God has said nothing since? The
unequivocal answer is that it is so. That does not at
all mean that men have understood all He then said.
The Church of God in its entirety has not fully
grasped all the height and depth of His teaching. For
nineteen hundred years the most wonderful attention
has been given to it; and yet it will readily be conceded
by those who have been most diligent in examination,
that, to employ the words of Robinson in this application, " There is yet much more light and truth to break
forth from the Word of God."

This appeal, then, in the closing movement of the
letter, " See that ye refuse not Him that speaketh,"
should ever be read in close connection with the opening statement:

> " God, having of old time spoken unto the fathers in
> the prophets by divers portions and in divers manners,
> hath at the end of these days spoken unto us in His
> Son."

Thus to bring the first and last together, in brief sentences, we may read:

> " God . . . hath . . . spoken unto us in His Son."
> " See that ye refuse not Him that speaketh."

Necessarily the writer is urging us to pay attention to

the message of Jesus, but we are to realize that that message is God's message to men. The truth is enforced in the words which follow:

> " For if they escaped not, when they refused him that warned in earth, much more shall not we escape, who turn away from Him that warneth from heaven."

Here once more the two movements of Divine revelation are referred to. In the first, God warned men on the earth level. In the final, He has spoken to men directly from heaven.

Referring to the past; in every method of God there had been some central principle, some central value of revelation. All these separated parts were now merged in the message of the Son. Nothing essential that God had said to man before the coming of Jesus was contradicted, or denied, or superseded. In Him everything was said again, but with new meaning, with new value, with added emphasis. It is poetry on the highest level, and yet clear revelation of insight and interpretation when John in the Apocalypse, describing the vision that was granted to him in Patmos, said among other things:

> " His voice as the voice of many waters."

Personally I never grasped the significance of that until I stood one day by the side of the Falls of Niagara, and listened to the waters. As I stood and listened I thought of whence those rushing waters came. I remembered the mountains lying behind, and all the rivulets and rills that were rising and racing down the

mountain sides, until presently merging, they became
a great river; and then other rills and other rivers,
waters, waters which at last poured themselves over in
the music of the mighty falls. The voice of many
waters. Thus I hear the speech of the Son, and in it
all the music of the flowing streams of the Old Testament merging into the full and final speech of God
through the Son.

In passing over the letter we have heard first the
speech of God through angelic ministry. Of course it
is impossible to deal with the details of the revelation
that came in that way, but we may gather up the whole
of the message through the angels, and declare that it
concerned the throne and government of Almighty
God. From the appearance of the cherubim at Eden's
gate to the testifying angels of the Apocalypse, the
message had always been concerned with the sovereignty of God. All that they said on that sublime
subject has been finally said and completely interpreted
in the message through the Son.

Next in order we come to Moses, who was the faithful servant in all the house. Through him we may
with equal brevity, and yet accuracy, declare that the
message was that of the supreme importance of law,
that is, the application of the Divine sovereignty to
all human affairs. All that God said to man through
Moses concerning the application of His sovereignty
through law to all the details of human life and conduct
was now said, perfectly, finally, completely, in the
ethical teaching of the Son.

Passing over the history we come to Joshua. We are

often inclined to think of him as a warrior, but he was
infinitely more, He was the captain of the hosts of the
Lord, those hosts who were called upon in the Divine
economy to cut out the cancer in the world's life, of a
corrupt people, and establish a centre of healing and
beneficent blessing. Through Joshua God was revealing to men the necessity for organization. The people
established in that little stretch of land, washed by the
waters of the Great Sea, in order to the fulfilment of
their mission, needed such leadership and such organization. The Son, when He spoke, revealed superlatively and finally the same necessity in the brief but
sublime things He said concerning His Church as to
the law of her life, and her activities.

Moreover, God had spoken through priesthood, with
Aaron as the great central personality. Following the
historic line we reach at this point the supreme need of
humanity. Rebels against the Divine sovereignty, careless about the Divine law, self-centred, rather than living in relationship with others, they needed supremely
mediation, some way of access to God. He gave them
a revealing ritual, the great value of which was not the
ritual, but the things it suggested.

All this is clearly brought forth in the history of the
past speech of God. If we watch the historian who
writes, or listen to the singer as he sings, and attend to
the prophets as they speak, God is ever speaking, and
the things He had to say to men concerned His sovereignty, the necessity for law, the necessity for true
organization, and the necessity for a way of approach
to Himself through mediation.

With this survey we may now declare that in the speech of God to men through the Son first we have nothing new. In all that He said there was nothing which He had not said before. The God Who had spoken in divers portions, divers manners, now through the Son said the same essential things about human life. It is quite possible that this statement may be challenged, that it is challengeable. Careful consideration, however, will show that it abides true. How often we have been told that through Jesus the one new thing about God made known was that of God's Fatherhood. Let us remember that a Hebrew singer had declared that:

> " Like as a father pitieth his children,
>   So the Lord pitieth them that fear Him."

We constantly use what we speak of as the Lord's Prayer without realizing that every sentence in it is really a quotation from Talmudic literature, saturated with previous Biblical literature.

Having said that, let us now make a further statement about the speech of the Son. Everything He said was new. He said the things which God had been saying through the ages, but now in such a way that men discovered, and have ever since been discovering, that they only commenced to understand the revelation of God as it was uttered in and through Him. The message of the angelic revelation of the sovereignty of God was now spoken so that it became an entirely new conception, whereas it was an eternal truth. The Son insisted upon the sovereignty of God as He said, " Seek

ye first the Kingdom of God," and interpreted that
sovereignty as He said, " God so loved the world that
He gave."

As to law, the Son distinctly declared:

" I came not to destroy the law, but to fulfil it."

When one day a man, whose profession was concerned
with the ancient law, asked Him, which is the great
commandment in the law? our Lord summarized everything in Moses by quoting from Moses, and adding to
the double quotation a word of practical importance.
From Moses He quoted:

" Thou shalt love the Lord thy God with all thy
heart, and with all thy soul, and with all thy mind."

Concerning that He declared it was " the great and
first commandment." That is to say, that there can be
no right relationship between God and man that is not
rooted in man's right relationship with Him. He then
declared a second, a sequence:

" Thou shalt love thy neighbour as thyself " ;

and finally added the great word:

" On these two commandments hangeth the whole
law, and the prophets."

The final interpretation of law is, of course, discovered
in the ethical manifesto of Jesus. Thus through Him
God said the old thing in such new form and fashion

as to emphasize the necessity of law, and to interpret its requirements.

When we come to Joshua and organization, we hear the voice of the Son saying:

" On this rock I will build *My* Church,"

My Ecclesia, *My* Theocracy,

" And the gates of Hades shall not prevail against it."

Thus, in the speech of God through the Son we have the statement concerning the one organization through which the sovereignty of God is to be proclaimed, and His law applied to human life.

God had spoken concerning mediation through priesthood, with Aaron as the central figure. He now spoke on that same fundamental necessity through a Priest after the order of Melchizedek. That Priest Himself upon occasion, said:

" No one cometh unto the Father but by Me,"

the inescapable implicate is that all men can reach the Father through Him.

Thus He Who had spoken in the past in divers portions and divers manners which had never been completely apprehended, nor indeed could have been, spoke at last through Him in Whom the many waters merge into the one Voice.

In view of all this the appeal of the writer,

" See that ye refuse not Him that speaketh,"

finds its full power. It was given to Hebrew Christians.
It remains the message to the Church. It is more than
that, because the outlook of this letter, and the outlook
of the speech of God to men is ever world-wide in its
intention and in its purpose.

Supposing that speech is refused, what then? There
is no need for any answer to be given to that inquiry
if we think of world conditions at the present moment.
What is the matter really with the whole world today?
The sovereignty of God is neglected, the law of God
is ignored, the methods of God are contemned, the
mediation of God is refused.

The result is that we have the vision of man, still
striving after the full realization of life individually,
socially, nationally, and never able to arrive. All this
because man cannot find an authority equal to the
management of human affairs. Monarchy has failed.
Democracy has broken down, and the world today is
facing dictators, and that is already seen to be facing
disaster.

The result of all this is that law breaks down. If we
refuse the interpretation of law found in the message
of the Son, we have nothing but failure. The laws that
men make are necessarily based upon the examination
of conditions, and these are constantly changing. The
laws of God deal with causes, and thus ensure full
realization.

Still thinking of the past and of organization, we
come to the Divine provision of the Church. Here, of
course, we have much to cause the heart sorrow, and
yet that institution which has brought all the things

into human life that are worth while is the Church. Where today it appears as though men were refusing the Church, careful consideration will show that they are not refusing the Church of God, but that Christendom which calls itself the Church, which has so largely failed. Nevertheless the inward, spiritual reality remains as the light of the world.

The final word therefore is the word of this appeal, because if we refuse the Son, there is no more a name given among men through whom salvation can come. That declaration fell from the lips of Peter as he addressed the early Church. It was arraigned and arrested before a rationalistic religion. The Sadducees had challenged the Church, and Peter then made this declaration:

> " He is the stone which was set at nought of you the builders, which was made the head of the corner. And in none other is there salvation; for neither is there any other name under heaven, that is given among men, wherein we must be saved."

That is a national, racial, human statement. It was indeed a remarkable statement as it declared that this One had been set aside by the builders, that is, by the experts. These had accounted Him to be " nought," a cipher. Peter declared that He was the chief Cornerstone. The architectural figure there, of course, is that of the pyramid. An examination of a pyramid will reveal the fact that the corner-stone is the key to the whole building, the stone from which you can find the height and breadth and dimensions thereof. Of human life in its saving and in its realization, the Son is the Corner-stone. Unless we build according to the lines revealed in Him, we shall never reach the triumphant apex, shall never have a perfect structure. While other voices, ten thousand of them, are clamouring for our attention, let us listen anew to the voice of God, and see to it that we " refuse not Him that speaketh."

XVI

THE UNCHANGING SON

" Jesus Christ is the same yesterday, and today, yea, and for ever."
—HEBREWS xiii. 8.

THE closing chapter of the letter to the Hebrews consists of injunctions and instructions based upon all the teaching that has preceded. Faith in God manifested as obedience to His revelation is seen to be the secret of life. God has spoken. Men have heard. When they have believed what God has had to say, whether in times past in divers portions and in divers manners through the prophets, or now in His final speech to man in His Son; and when they have believed with the belief that produces obedience, they have found the secret of life.

In the midst of those closing instructions and injunctions, with none of which I propose to deal, this great declaration of the writer is found:

" Jesus Christ is the same yesterday, and today, yea, and for ever " ;

or slightly to change the reading:

" Jesus Christ is the same yesterday, and today, yea, and unto the ages."

This is the ultimate statement in the book as to the finality of what God has said to men in His Son. There can be no change, because He is changeless. While referring to Him " today," the writer links the statement with the past " yesterday," and with all the future, " unto the ages." The reference to " yesterday " includes not merely the period of God's speech to men, but the far-flung mystery of which we can only speak as ages past. The reference to the future shows that in Him all life is to be conditioned not here and now alone, but in all the mystery of that which is to come, " unto the ages."

In dealing with this statement we take for our divisions the simple thoughts suggested by these phrases; Jesus Christ yesterday, Jesus Christ today, Jesus Christ for ever.

Here we pause briefly to notice definitely how the writer refers to the Son of God at this point, as he speaks of Him as " Jesus Christ." There is no carelessness by these New Testament writers in the use of a name or a title at any point. Here, as in the Old Testament, we find no carelessness in the particular name of God employed at any point. As we have taken our way through the letter we have found the Son of God referred to in different ways. He is called " The Son." That is the great introductory word, when declaring that God had spoken to us in " a Son." Eight times over in the course of the letter does he thus refer to Him. Four times he distinctly calls Him " the Son of God." Thrice he designates Him " the Lord." Eight times he uses the human name alone, " Jesus."

Once he links that name with the title, " the Lord
Jesus." Eight times he employs the Messianic title,
" Christ." Three times he employs the formula of this
statement, linking the name with the title, " Jesus
Christ." Four times he refers to " the Word of God."
Whatever the title may be, the Person is ever before
the mind, but every name has some distinctive value
at the moment it is employed.

Here, as we have said, he joins a name and a title
which he has done on two other occasions, once when
declaring that the Son is the One through Whom the
will of God for our sanctification is accomplished, once
where he declared that the Son is over His own House.
Here then we find the titles together once more. The
name, so sacred and so familiar, Jesus, is used. Very
little need be said about that.

> " Jesus, Name of sweetness,
>   Jesus, sound of love;
>   Cheering exiles onward
>   To their rest above.
>
>   Jesus, oh the magic
>   Of the soft love sound,
>   How it thrills and trembles
>   To creation's bound."

It is a peculiarly human name, yet full of profound
significance, a name which, according to the records,
was first borne by the man who succeeded Moses, and
was given to him by Moses; a name in which certain
parts of the Divine name, Yahweh, and certain parts

of this man's original name Hoshea, were linked together. Its significance then is that of salvation by Jehovah. Said the angel:

> "Thou shalt call His name JESUS, for it is He that shall save His people from their sins."

It is inevitable, however, that when we use the name our attention is fastened upon the human. In this writing this name does not emerge until we reach the second chapter and the ninth verse. We have first the whole of the introduction, fastening attention upon the glory of the Person of the Son. Then says the writer:

> "We behold Him Who hath been made a little lower than the angels, even Jesus."

When we turn to the title "Christ," we find that it is not employed by the writer until we reach chapter three and verse six:

> "Christ as a Son, over His House; Whose House are we."

Now, says the writer, "Jesus Christ is the same yesterday, and today, and unto the ages." This Person is defined for us by a name that brings Him into closest association with our human nature, the name He bore in the days of His flesh, the name which nevertheless has significance concerning the meaning and purpose of His incarnation, "Thou shalt call His name JESUS."

He is, moreover, entitled "Christ," the Messiah, the One Who is at once King and Priest, Whose crown of kingship is a mitre of priesthood, Whose ephod of priesthood is purple in royalty. That is the One concerning Whom the writer makes the declaration that He is " the same yesterday, today, and unto the ages."

The Person introduced, then, is according to the opening of the letter a Son, Heir of all things, through Whom God fashioned the ages, the Effulgence of the Divine glory, the very Image of the Divine substance, Who upholds all things by the word of His power, and Who made purification for sins. This is Jesus, Whom men observed, and heard speak with a human voice, and He is the Christ.

If, then, we would apprehend the great declaration we are considering, we realize that the focal point of revelation is found as we look at Him as He was in the " yesterday " of time. The central facts of God, and of our own nature are utterly beyond the possibility of our complete apprehension or understanding. That, of course, is the meaning of the Incarnation. It was that John had in his mind when he wrote:

> " The Word became flesh, and tabernacled among us . . . and we beheld."

The Eternal had in Jesus temporal manifestation. The Infinite Logos came to the level where it was possible for finite eyes to behold, and by such beholding to be introduced to the infinite things themselves.

We will look at Him then in the midst of that period of manifestation, the days of His flesh. This necessarily means we must consult the records. Going back, then, to the Gospel narratives we inquire, How do we

see Him?   This is an easy question to ask, but an
impossible one to answer with adequacy.   Nevertheless
there are certain outstanding facts which are full of
value.

As we behold Him there, we see One Whose appeal
was ever made to essential humanity, quite apart from
any racial position, or privilege, or limitation, or dis-
advantage.   An illustration of what I mean is an old
and familiar one, but nevertheless pertinent.   Many
years ago there was an exhibition in London of Tissot's
pictures, about 270 of them, illustrative of the earthly
life of Jesus.   There is much in them that does not
appeal, but there is one outstanding fact, and it is
that, while the artist depicts with accuracy the setting
of the story, and the customs of the time, so that as we
look we can racially place the Roman patrician or
plebeian, the cultured Greek, the barbarian, and the
Jew, he never painted the face of Jesus so that it could
be thus placed.   Now literally he may have been wrong.
It is possible that our Lord had the distinct face of the
Jew, though we have no means of proving it.   But it is
certainly spiritually correct.   Paul understood the great
truth when he wrote:

" There can be neither Jew nor Greek, there can be
neither bond nor free, there can be no male or female;
for ye are all one in Christ Jesus."

All the things by which we place individuals so as to
mark their separation from others, are absent.   It
was in this way He made His constant appeal to men,

and attracted them towards Him. It was not the
teaching of Jesus that appealed to men. They refused
it. They knew it was true, and that was why they
objected to it, because the truth condemned them. As
long as Savonarola said to Florence, " Be free," they
applauded him; but when he said, " Be pure," they
refused him. Jesus said, Be pure from first to last.
Therefore His teaching did not appeal. But His
humanity did. He was irresistible. It is impossible
to read the narratives without hearing the tramp of the
crowds following Him, the common people, which does
not mean the people of what we sometimes call the
lower orders, but of all orders. Men found in Him a
merging of grace and truth, sweetness and strength,
meekness and majesty, light and love. " Yesterday,"
then, He appealed to men by His sheer humanity. The
truth abides today.

In the title " Christ " we have a recognition of the
appeal He made to humanity in its need. For the
purpose of our present study we may say that humanity's need is revealed in the use of two words, sin and
sorrow. Sorrow is the result of sin. We watch Him
then in the world where sin and sorrow abound. With
regard to sin we see that He never excused it. We
speak today of " necessary evils." Such a phrase never
passed His lips, for such a thought never occupied His
mind. It is indeed a contradiction of terms according
to Him. What is necessary cannot be evil. What is
evil can never be necessary.

But again. If He never excused sin, He never aban-
doned the sinner. We will take another phrase that we

are apt to use, " a hopeless case." That phrase, moreover, never passed His lips, because it had no place in
His thinking. There were no hopeless cases as He
looked at men. The story of His dealings with men and
women reveals what in a proper and guarded sense we
may refer to as His magnificent optimism in the presence of all human dereliction. However evil a man
might be, however low a woman might have sunk, He
treated them as salvable.

When we turn to sorrow, He was Himself a Man of
sorrows, and acquainted with grief, and in His dealing
with others He never ignored sorrow; but neither for
Himself nor for others did He submit to it. He never
treated it as something which should fill men with
despair. Just as He was leaving His disciples He said
this remarkable thing to them, " Your sorrow shall be
turned into joy." Let this be carefully noted, that He
did not say, Your sorrow shall have compensating joy,
but rather that the sorrow in itself should be transmuted into joy.

Thus we see Him " yesterday," appealing to humanity by the essentials of His own humanity, and facing the conditions of sin and sorrow, never excusing
the sin or abandoning the sinner, never ignoring sorrow
or admitting that it was the final word.

Still looking on that " yesterday " we see that He
was ever creating in the minds of those about Him new
surprise. Ever and anon there broke from Him, in
some act or word or attitude something that amazed
His followers, something for which they could not
account. It may safely be declared that He trained

His disciples by surprising them step by step. Such is an incomplete and inadequate attempt to glance back to the " yesterday " on the human level.

The writer of the declaration affirms that He is the same " today," that is, the same in these essential matters. We realize that there is a difference between " today " and " yesterday." In the days of His flesh He was localized and limited by such localization. Knowing this, ere He left His disciples He said to them:

> " It is expedient for you that I go away, for if I go not away, the Comforter will not come unto you."

He is no longer with us as He was with those early disciples in bodily form, but in all the essential things that found manifestation then He is with us still. We know Him through the writings. In these we have the account of Him in germ, by which, of course, I mean it needs elaboration, application, contemplation. But He is found in the Gospels not only in germ, but in norm. That is to say, all our thinking must for ever be conditioned by their revelation. Here is the point in which much attempted interpretation of Jesus Christ, and of His message, fails. A Person adapted to a natural philosophy is not the Person of the Gospels. In the Gospels we find the One Who gave the world its final ethic, and its only evangel. If we change the Person we lower the ethic, and destroy the evangel.

Briefly we may apply the things considered. He still appeals to humanity. When Jesus is revealed, apart from ecclesiasticism and secularism, He remains as attractive to human nature as He was in the days of His flesh. Let the simple story be told, and whether they obey or not, men see the beauty of the Person.

He remains, moreover, the same in His attitude towards sin. He never excuses it, and hypocrisy is impossible in His presence. Perhaps the chief and most radiant glory is the fact that He is the same in that He does not abandon us if we have sinned. He is still saying to all critical, cold, callous moralists, Let him that is without sin cast a stone at this sinning woman. Moreover, He is still the same in His attitude towards sorrow. He never ignores it. If Mary is weeping at His feet for her dead brother, He will weep with her, even though He is Master of life and death. As Faber wrote:

> " In every pang that rends the heart,
> The Man of Sorrows has His part."

And yet again, the same mysteries abide. He cannot be finally placed. All human examinations have failed to do that. No decade has passed but that some light that had never before been apprehended, has broken upon some devout student of the Christ, and found expression in some interpretation.

Once glance at the " for ever," or " unto the ages." I prefer this more literal translation because it attempts no mathematical measurement. It is poetically suggestive. We refer to the ages, and our thinking follows as far as is possible, and then reverently halts. It ever seems to me that the strongest expression concerning

Eternity in the New Testament came from the pen of Paul when he wrote, " unto the generation of the age of the ages." The ages come, and they pass, each having its own nature, its own period of duration, its own peculiar forces and values. Paul seems to see them all generated, or born in succession, and encompassed into one age. This is the phrase employed by the writer, when looking into the future he declares that Jesus Christ is the same. At the beginning of the letter he had declared the ages were fashioned through the Son. He now affirms that through them all He remains the same. Whatever the future may have in store therefore, He will ever be the Revealer of truth, and the Manifester of grace. All the unfathomed deeps and distances are seen in Him.

Through Him God has spoken to man, and He has nothing more to say. There is no need for more. There is need that we should understand what He said in the Son more perfectly, and so grow up into Him in all things in knowledge and experience.

Change; we are all conscious of change. It is at once the salt and the poison of life. As salt, it prevents corruption. If we knew nothing of change along the level of our human experience it would indeed be a terrible thing. The Psalmist once said of the wicked, " They have no changes." But it is also the very poison of life, as it seems to interfere with our arrangements, and apparently with our progress. It is out of the poignant sense of this that the singer sang:

" Change and decay in all around I see."

But observe carefully that this statement was made to lead to the great appeal:

" O Thou Who changest not, abide with me."

In all human life we need a centre of permanence, that to which we can fasten our lives, and know that it abides. We also need a secret of perennial freshness. Both are found in Him. I change, He changes not. Moreover, He is the Secret of perennial freshness. There is never a day in the loneliness of our own situation when, if we abide in Him, He does not break upon us with some new glory, some new beauty.

Thus the final word of God to men is spoken in a Son, Jesus Christ, Who is " the same yesterday, today, and unto the ages."

Made in the USA
Monee, IL
29 December 2022